The Aerofilms Book of
BRITAIN'S RAILWAYS
FROM THE AIR

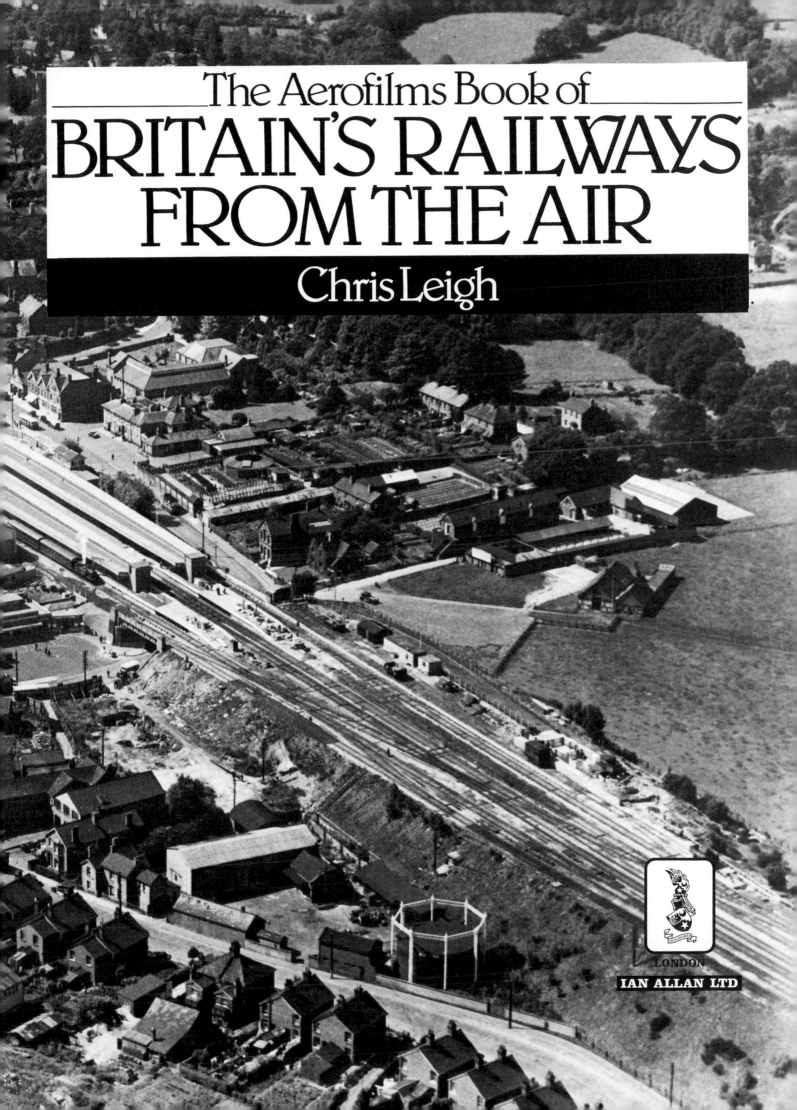

The Aerofilms Book of
BRITAIN'S RAILWAYS
FROM THE AIR

Chris Leigh

LONDON

IAN ALLAN LTD

First published 1987
Reprinted 1988

ISBN 0 7110 1702 6

 Photographs © Aerofilms Ltd 1987

Text © Ian Allan Ltd 1987

Published by Ian Allan Ltd, Shepperton, Surrey;
and printed by Ian Allan Printing Ltd at their works
at Coombelands in Runnymede, England

Contents

Jacket cover, front:
The 1987 railway in a rural setting. An IC125 unit forming a Paddington-Plymouth express runs at full speed through the countryside near Frome.
CT16812

Jacket cover, back:
On the preserved Bluebell Railway between Sheffield Park and Horsted Keynes, ex-South Eastern & Chatham Railway 'C' class 0-6-0 No 592 heads the breakdown train through rural Sussex.
AC437336

End-papers:
A perpendicular view of York on 23 August 1936. Bottom right, Y&NM original station (closed 1877), above it the present station and, bottom centre, the roundhouses. Centre right, the River Ouse with the locomotive depot, now the National Railway Museum, alongside. Left, York carriage workshops.
SV7603

Title page:
Haywards Heath.

Dedication
For Diane;
and in admiration of the photographers and aviators of Aerofilms and its constituents.

Acknowledgement
Sincere thanks are due to Aerofilms' Chief Librarian, Peter O'Connell, for his diligent research and assistance, and to other members of the Aerofilms staff.

Preface: Aerofilms

An insignificant building on a trading estate at Elstree houses one of the most remarkable historic photograph collections in the UK. The Aerofilms' library contains more than half a million photographs dating from around 1920 to the present day. The landscape, rural and urban, is shown from an aerial viewpoint which gives an instant appreciation of the form and layout of our environment, which cannot readily be demonstrated by any other means.

How did Aerofilms begin? The company was founded in May 1919 by F. L. Wills who had been a photographer with the Royal Flying Corps during World War 1. Seeing the commercial possibilities of aerial photography, he abandoned his war-interrupted career as an architect to become managing director, with Claude Graham-White as Chairman.

Although photography had been invented a century earlier, the equipment and the aircraft were primitive by modern standards. Some of the early hand-held cameras were of wooden construction and all were plate cameras until the mid to late 1920s when cut film or roll film was used. The 'P' type Aero (plate) camera, made by R. W. Munro of London, was typical of the early cameras used by Aerofilms. First introduced during World War 1 in the RNAS and later in the RAF, it had fixed cones for 8½in and 10½in lenses, a focal plane shutter and took 5in×4in

Below:
Preparing for a photographic sortie in 1919. The pilot, Mr Shaw occupies the centre cockpit of the converted de Havilland DH9, while F. L. Wills is seen in the front, and Mr Freise-Green clasps his heavy plate camera in the rear position. **C12930**

Above:
An Aerofilms photographer poses for the camera during the early 1930s, before climbing into the open cockpit of his Klemm L25 monoplane. **B1264**

glass negatives which had to be individually loaded into the camera for each exposure. The early aircraft were open-seater biplanes, the first sorties being flown in a converted DH9 on contract from the Aircraft Operating Co. Among the early pilots were Harry Hawker and Alan Cobham (later Sir Alan) who flew for Aerofilms in the early 1920s. Another pioneer who was associated with Aerofilms was Freise-Green who joined as an air photographer in 1919 when the company was engaged for the flying sequences in the production of weekly silent movie thrillers.

In 1921 Aerofilms was involved in the first test case under the Air Navigation Regulations when Wills and pilot Capt Olley force-landed in a pond in Southwark Park. Aerofilms continued to clock up 'firsts' in the various activities in which they became involved; in 1920 the first air survey was completed in the form of photo-mosaics of scaled vertical photographs of Finchley. This was followed in 1921 by aerial photography for a traffic survey for the Metropolitan Police. In 1925 the Ordnance Survey commissioned a trial aerial survey of Eastbourne, for whilst the Aerofilms library rapidly filled with oblique aerial photographs, Wills always had his eye on the newly developing science of photogrammetry, the art of producing maps from vertical photographs, which led to the purchase in 1938 of a Swiss Wild A5 stereo plotting instrument — the first of its kind in the country.

Both the financial holdings of Aerofilms and the premises from which Wills and his trail-blazers worked, changed a number of times during the inter-war period.

He had started in 1919 with a bathroom and office in the London Aerodrome, Hendon, and later moved on to a palatial mansion in the Edgware Road in 1924. In 1928 Aerofilms established itself in its first real factory in Colindale Avenue. Meanwhile it had come under the wing of the Aircraft Operating Co of London which had survey contracts in southern Africa. After a period with the offices at Bush House in the Aldwych, the company moved back to northwest London taking a factory at Stonebridge Park, Wembley. In 1938, the Hunting Group became a shareholder in the Aircraft Operating Co, and in 1943 Hunting secured full control.

After World War 2 Wills became managing director of both the survey company and Aerofilms; he retired in 1958. Another early aerial photographer, who joined the company in 1922, was C. E. Murrell, who was trained by Wills. Murrell left in 1934 to form his own company, Aero Pictorial, which became a major rival but was eventually merged with Aerofilms.

Over the years many interesting contracts and experiences have come Aerofilms' way. One of the first official contracts called for monthly photography to record the builiding of the Wembley Exhibition from 1922 to its opening in 1924. In 1924, Wills was interviewed by Scotland Yard who confiscated some aerial photographs, and threatened him with prison unless his over-enthusiastic photographers paid heed to the Official Secrets Act! Later, in the early 1930s, someone accused Aerofilms of photographing the roof tops of country houses to aid cat burglars!

Today Aerofilms contracts for photographic sorties still take in large estates and country houses, but increasingly the work is angled towards major construction sites, motorways, developments, town planning and surveying. Since the early 1970s the company's range of colour material has steadily increased, prompting demands from publishers for illustrative material. Modern photographic materials and aircraft have taken a lot of the uncertainty out of the job, but weather conditions and special assignments can still produce a challenge to test the skill of the company whose publicity boldly claims: 'We photograph anything, anywhere, from the air'.

Introduction

I first encountered Aerofilms as a teenager, in the 1960s, when researching the Wellington-Much Wenlock branch in connection with a proposed model railway layout. I cannot remember where I first saw the name, but I suspect it was in a small advertisement in one of the railway magazines. I was seeking pictures of Buildwas station and an application to Aerofilms brought forth a speedy response with several views of the Severn Valley in that area, but all concentrating on the power station or the Abbey ruins. If only one of them had included the station, it would have solved all my problems. From that point I became aware of the value of aerial photography.

I had never imagined that I would be asked to produce a book based on Aerofilms' material, and when the offer came, the prospect was rather daunting. The photographs comprise a vast selection, taken all over the British Isles from July 1919 up to date, mainly in connection with mapping work, planning or commercial development. Consequently, it represents the accumulation of thousands of different jobs and individual aerial sorties each with a different specific purpose. It is, therefore, not a comprehensive geographical coverage. There may be a dozen shots of a specific location, and not one of another area close by. In other areas, 15 counties have complete coverage.

A preliminary selection had already been made, by extracting the majority of prints which featured a railway subject fairly prominently. Two boxes of such prints were passed to me and from that point the job became a three-cornered exercise. Firstly, the selection had to be whittled down to around 150 illustrations which would actually be used. Secondly, those pictures had to be grouped into chapters under suitable headings. Finally, each one had to be identified and captioned.

In reducing the selection to manageable proportions I eliminated many prints which were too dark, blurred, or not specifically taken with the railway as the main feature. I then identified instances where there were several views of the same subject and selected the best single print from each of these.

I thus arrived at a totally miscellaneous collection of railway views, and much time was spent sorting them into the various categories. It quickly became apparent that even-handed geographical coverage would be out of the question. Some areas faired much better than others. I make no apology for the choice, since the subjects were a *fait accompli*. No one wishes more than I, that I could turn back the clock and send that photographer up to photograph some of the locations that he missed.

What has survived the selection process is without doubt a worthy collection of views. From 1,000ft above the ground, the camera takes in a large area of the land beneath, and many of these views are pictures of the ever-varied British landscape in which the railway is the linking feature. I hope it will prove to be of interest to readers other than railway buffs and that is why some of the captions and introductory paragraphs set out to explain aspects of railway practice.

The period covered by the illustrations embraces more than five decades, commencing around 1920. It is well worth noting the exceptionally high quality of some of the earliest views. One can imagine the cumbersome glass-plate camera, presumably attached fairly precariously to the open cockpit of some vibrating biplane, for at that time photography was less in its infancy than aviation, but neither could be said to be technologically advanced. In today's world, where subjects no bigger than a bus can be photographed clearly from a satellite outside the Earth's atmosphere, we can but pause to admire the combined efforts of these early aviators and photographers who had to be up there doing their job, rather than sitting in an office doing it by remote control.

This book is as much about the landscape around the railway as about the railway itself. The research has been fascinating. The prints have the barest of captions — sometimes a place and date, others just a place, or nothing at all. Occasionally, the stated location has proved to be incorrect. The detective work has been enjoyable, but if I have been mistaken in some aspect of a caption, the mistake is my own. In one or two instances an illustration was

Dawlish, 1932

It would be difficult to find a station closer to the beach than that at Dawlish, seen here in the summer of 1932. Brunel's sea wall route along this stretch of the South Devon coast is one of the most photographed sections of railway, but it is not usually seen from the air. The sea looks benign enough here, but whipped to a frenzy by winter storms it has been a constant source of trouble and expense. **39683**

omitted because it proved impossible to pin down sufficient information to caption it. In other instances I have stated clearly where something is believed to be true but where there is no means of being certain. The reader may well find large-scale maps and a good quality magnifier helpful for studying pictures in detail.

Aerofilms employs two techniques of aerial photography, perpendicular — used mainly for map work, and oblique — for general purposes. Virtually all the illustrations herein are oblique. They vary in height from the very low views like the one of the LMS Beyer-Garratt locomotive, up to perhaps 2,000ft above the ground.

Aerofilms' work is carried out mainly for architects, planning officers and commercial concerns. Such work is skilled and expensive and the company's prints are priced accordingly. At present rates, a single 10in×8in print from the original negative would cost more than the price of this book.

I hope that in assembling this work I have produced an album worthy of the skilled and professional efforts of those who made the original pictures. I trust that it will appeal not just to the railway enthusiast, but to the casual reader, the social and environmental historian, and to those who just want a unique viewpoint on the way things used to be.

Chris Leigh   Old Windsor
                                                            1987

London

The multitude of railway companies which sought to serve London left a legacy of remarkable station architecture and some of the finest railway station structures in the world. Such was the spirit of conflict and competition between them that they also left London without a major through station, and apart from round-about routes such as the North London line or the West London line, it remains impossible at the time of writing to cross the capital by a main line passenger train.

In this chapter I have endeavoured to include all the major termini — and at least one from each of the Regions, although as will be seen, some areas are much better covered than others. I have also included one or two oddities to illustrate that London's railways were not all major passenger terminals.

Clapham Junction, 1948

No selection of railway scenes in London would be complete without a picture of Clapham Junction. The station is seen in the centre, with the lines into Waterloo and Victoria at the top. The lines to Victoria are on the right, and diverge to rise up and cross over the Waterloo lines. To the right of the Victoria lines, further tracks diverge to pass under the Waterloo lines to reach Latchmere Junction and the West London line. The station has two distinct sections, the platforms at left serving the 'Windsor lines' to Reading, and those on the right serving the ex-LSWR main line to the west, and the ex-LBSCR Brighton line. Several electric multiple-unit trains can be seen and there is much stabled coaching stock including several Pullman cars for Boat Trains to Southampton. **57013**

Brentford, 1947

A fine view of the 'ribbon' industrial development which sprang up on the major roads radiating from London. This is the Great West Road (A4) in 1937, crossed by the Great Western Railway branch from Southall to Brentford. The branch had closed to passenger services a few years previously, and here a 0-6-0PT is leaving Brentford with a freight train. The goods yard is off the picture to the right, but the signalbox and some sidings can be seen. The bridge was removed in the 1970s and the branch now finishes just on the right of the main road, where it serves a stone depot and refuse container terminal. The magnificent art deco Firestone building was demolished a few years ago amid a storm of protest and the elevated section of the M4 motorway now cuts through the background of this picture. **R2624**

Crystal Palace, 1928

The magnificent Crystal Palace was constructed in Hyde Park for the Great Empire Exhibition of 1851. Bringing together all the great designers and engineers of its day, it featured the work of Paxton, Matthew Digby Wyatt, and water towers by Brunel. It was subsequently re-erected at the south London site which took its name, and was destroyed by fire in 1936. This fine 1928 view shows the 'back' of the Palace, with the High Level station, served by the branch from Nunhead (closed 1954) hidden immediately beyond it. The Low Level terminus, served from Sydenham, is seen bottom left, in its later state with roof removed. Below it, the line from Norwood Junction to Tulse Hill enters its tunnel under the Palace.   **C13212**

St Pancras & King's Cross, 1957

The Midland Railway's St Pancras terminus and the Great Northern Railway's King's Cross stand side by side, presenting a stark contrast in architectural styles. Fronted by the Midland Grand Hotel, later turned into ofices, St Pancras was started in 1866 when the Midland decided that it must have its own independent access to London. The construction involved eviction without compensation, of thousands of slum dwellers in Agar Town and Somers Town, and the upheaval of a burial ground with consequent repulsive working conditions. William Barlow's great single-span train shed roof is 689ft long, 245ft wide and stands at its apex 100ft above the rails. The tracks are some 20ft above street level, the ramps providing an imposing approach to the elaborate decorated frontage designed by Sir George Gilbert Scott. The structure was completed in 1873 and contained some 400 rooms. Despite its later conversion for use as offices, some features such as the grand staircase with its original carpet, remain. Electrification to Bedford has brought 25kV catenary into the station.

Opened in 1852 on the site of former smallpox and fever hospitals, King's Cross comprises two long narrow train sheds with a simple glazed screen and clock tower at the street end. This simple frontage has somehow managed to avoid becoming dated, and in the 1960s the clutter of buildings seen in front of it in this 1957 view, were replaced by a modern booking hall and improved station facilities. The modest Great Northern Hotel is seen to the left of the station frontage, and beyond it is the small and untidy King's Cross suburban station. Immediately beyond the station the tracks enter the 528yd Gasworks Tunnel, which takes them under the Regents Canal, visible above the tunnel portals. At top right is the vast King's Cross goods yard, most of which has now gone, while bottom left is the Midland's Somers Town goods yard, also now gone and being redeveloped. **A69826**

Above:
The magnificent frontage of St Pancras station in a view dating from the 'between the wars' period, which also shows part of King's Cross in the right-hand background. The board proclaiming the details of Somers Town goods depot is visible at bottom left. *Ian Allan Library*

King's Cross, 1957

Another view of the King's Cross and St Pancras area, this time looking more towards the east. At the very top, centre, is HM Prison, Pentonville, and below it, the Copenhagen Tunnel on the approach to King's Cross station. On emerging from the tunnel the tracks give access to the goods yard and 'Top Shed' (centre right, in the picture) while the main lines plunge almost immediately into Gasworks Tunnel. Immediately this side of 'Top Shed', an LMS 4-6-0 runs light along the line into St Pancras, while (centre) a tank locomotive shunts its goods train in the sidings east of Camden Town station. A great deal can be discovered by 'reading' these pictures in conjunction with a large scale street plan such as an *A to Z* atlas. This is a 1957 view.

67813

King's Cross, 1958

The camera is looking southwards in this view of the approaches to King's Cross and
St Pancras. The two termini are seen at the top left, with the entrance to Somers Town goods
depot top centre. The North London line runs across the bottom of the picture, and in the
centre lies the King's Cross goods yard and the locomotive depot, known as 'Top Shed'. The
pollution produced by some two dozen locomotives in steam tends to obscure the shed area,
but we can identify a number of Gresley Pacifics, including at least one 'A4'. The Regents
Canal sweeps round beyond the goods yard passing under the track approaching St Pancras
and over those outside King's Cross. Note in the goods yard the rake of identical open
wagons, all with their drop doors open and their insides swept clean. Also, the long shed
which houses some of the vast fleet of road vehicles engaged on local delivery work.   **A72115**

City of London, 1950

A fascinating view of the City in 1950, again showing two termini, with London Bridge station in the centre, and Cannon Street, top right. The complex of trackwork outside London Bridge is being threaded by a four-car suburban electric unit. It is only five years since the end of the war and widespread bomb damage is still evident in roofless buildings and empty sites. St Paul's Cathedral dominates Cannon Street station which has itself lost much of its roof covering — the metal ball finial from one of the towers was recovered from the river and set back in place in 1986. The bridges are, from the right, London Bridge, Cannon Street Railway Bridge, Southwark Bridge, Blackfriars Railway Bridge and Blackfriars Bridge. Note, at bottom right, the tramway tracks in the street. Tram services in London ended about one year later.

13401

City of London, 1929

Another interesting illustration of the City, dating from 1929, with the Pool of London (right) and Cannon Street station and Southwark Bridge (left). The triangle of tracks entering Cannon Street are formed by Borough Market Junction (right) and Metropolitan Junction (left). The station, and its approach engineering, were designed by John Hawkshaw and opened in 1866 to give the South Eastern Railway a terminus right in the City. Bombing during the Blitz and after caused extensive damage in the area, the station itself being badly affected on the night of 10/11 May 1941. Amid falling debris, railwaymen pulled trains out on to the bridge to save them, only to be bombed again in their exposed position. The roof was never again able to bear the weight of glass, and in the late 1950s it was dismantled. Later the buildings fronting the street were demolished and replaced with modern office blocks. Since it deals almost entirely with commuter traffic, the station has, for the past 30 years, been closed on Sundays.

28621

Above:
Dismantling of the overall roof at Cannon Street had commenced when this photograph was taken on 30 May 1958. 'Schools' class 4-4-0 No 30913 *Christs Hospital* is departing with the 5.06pm train to Hastings, while rebuilt 'West Country' 4-6-2 No 34025 *Whimple* waits with the 5.14pm to Ramsgate. *R. C. Riley*

19

Waterloo, 1958

Two London termini are seen in this view looking northwards from Waterloo across the Thames to the Victoria Embankment and the South Eastern & Chatham Railway's Charing Cross terminus, in 1958. The first Waterloo station opened in 1848, but by piecemeal development it became a ramshackle affair and in 1900 work started on the construction of the present 21-platform terminus designed by J. W. Jacomb-Hood and based on American practice of the time. It was opened in stages between 1909-11. In this view the Windsor lines are at the far side, with 4-SUB electric units in evidence. The main lines occupy the centre, with an 'M7' 0-4-4T on carriage shunting duties, and a rebuilt Bulleid 4-6-2 in view, and nearest the camera a Portsmouth electric unit, with roof destination boards in place. The building under construction by McAlpine is the Shell Centre, and to its right the Royal Festival Hall of 1951 can be seen. The road bridge is Waterloo Bridge, and to its left Hungerford Bridge carries the tracks into Charing Cross. This bridge also carries a pedestrian footpath which is a pleasant way to cross the river and see the trains. Charing Cross serves local and main line trains to north and east Kent. **A80041**

Below:
The last days of steam working from Waterloo. On a June evening in 1967 'Merchant Navy' 4-6-2 No 35013, formerly named *Blue Funnel*, sets out from the London terminus with a train for Salisbury. In the background a 'Warship' class diesel waits with an Exeter train. Steam working on the Southern Region ended in July 1967. *Ian Krause*

Liverpool Street, 1950s

A 1950s era view of the Great Eastern Railway's Liverpool Street terminus with the North London Railway's Broad Street, alongside it on the left. Top right, in this view, is Spitalfields Market, and the curved buildings at bottom left are in Finsbury Circus. In the league table of train arrivals, Broad Street was once third, exceeded only by Liverpool Street and Victoria. It was built with the support of the London & North Western Railway to provide them with a station in the City, but its architectural character never lived up to its importance in traffic terms. In 1968 its train shed roof was removed and by the 1980s only the North London line service to Richmond used the station. With the redevelopment of Liverpool Street in progress, Broad Street has disappeared for ever.

The main section of Liverpool Street station as seen in this view was opened in 1875, the design and construction being by Samuel Swarbrick who cared rather more for cost than aesthetic considerations and adopted a plan by which the platforms were below street level. A number of individual office buildings surround the train shed, which looks far more imposing from inside than out. In the early 1980s a plan for the reconstruction of the station was finally agreed, and work has commenced.　　　**A69827**

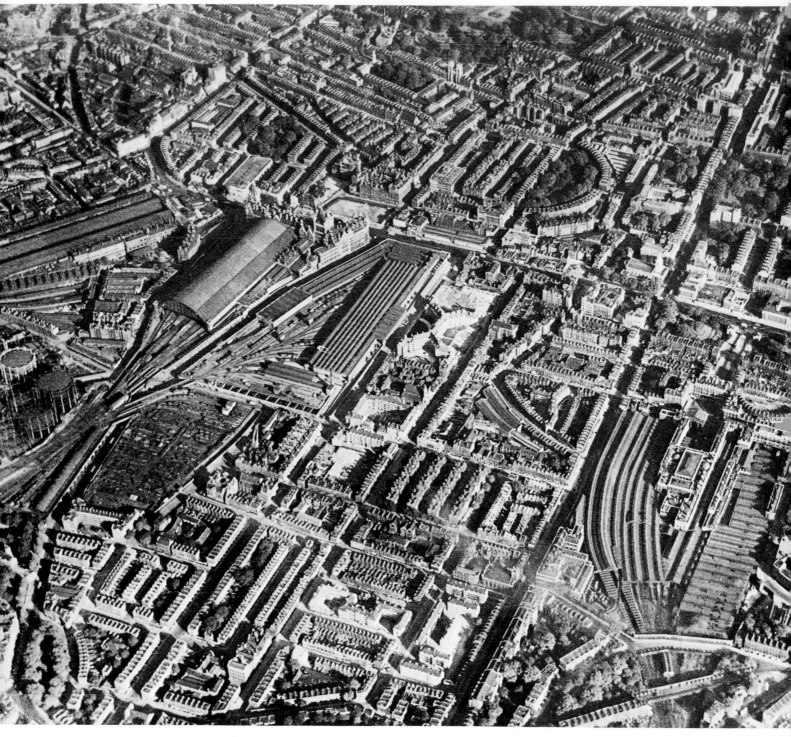

Euston, 1932

High above Euston in 1932, the Aerofilms photographer has captured three major termini in a single view. Bottom right is the Euston terminus of the London & North Western Railway. At the centre is St Pancras with Somers Town goods depot alongside, and on the left is King's Cross. Euston was London's first main line terminus, a grand affair planned by Robert Stephenson with architecture by Philip Hardwick. It opened in 1838. This view shows clearly how the siting of the Great Hall (built 1846-9) split the station in two and prevented effective development of the site when successive enlargements were required. The hall was elaborately decorated and cost £150,000. In the period up to World War 1, gradual enlargement and piecemeal additions enveloped Hardwick's original station and the whole place became unattractive and uninviting.

39587

Euston, 1936

A close-up of Euston from the road frontage showing the great hall with glazed domes on either side. The main platforms have been squeezed in on the right, with suburban platforms to the left. The great external feature of the original station was the 72ft-high portico which was completed in 1838 at a cost of £35,000. Its four hollow columns were 42ft high and 8ft 6in in diameter. It, too, became increasingly surrounded by development and by the time of this photograph it had become smoke-blackened and scruffy. Reconstruction of Euston was considered as early as the 1930s, but it was not until the electrification programme of 30 years later that it actually happened. Amid a huge outcry at the loss of the great Hall and Portico, Taylor Woodrow commenced reconstruction of the station in 1962. It was suggested that the Portico — the 'Doric Arch' as it had become known — could be moved on rollers to a new site, but nothing came of this and it was demolished, the stone apparently being cut up to make fireplaces or used as infill at Heathrow Airport.   **49739**

Right:
A fine interior view of Euston showing platforms 5-7 in about 1948, with fourth rail electrification visible and a Watford train standing on the right. *British Railways*

Above right:
Euston in 1953 with the Doric portico floodlit and the station decorated for the Coronation. *British Railways*

Paddington, 1946

A splendid view of Paddington, with the terminus station fronted by the Great Western Royal Hotel. On the left the tree-lined avenue of Westbourne Terrace is prominent, with Eastbourne Terrace at the centre of the picture, alongside the station. The three original curved roof sections show clearly, with the suburban section to their right. Beyond the station is Paddington goods depot, now cleared for redevelopment. The Paddington Basin of the Grand Union Canal shows as a dark area to the right of the station.　　　**A550**

Victoria, 1935

In this 1935 view of Victoria all those who possess that inbuilt, mysterious affection for our capital city will wish to look first at the background. From the top right corner, we see the Houses of Parliament and Westminster Abbey, with Westminster Bridge and Lambeth Bridge beyond. In the middle, top, we can just discern Admiralty Arch and we can then follow The Mall through the trees to the Queen Victoria Memorial and Buckingham Palace, where our unique viewpoint gives a glimpse of the Palace rear, and the gardens. Immediately below the Palace is Victoria station, its Brighton (left) and South Eastern (right) sections, distinctively different. Reached over the 930ft-long Grosvenor Bridge, Victoria's Brighton line section opened in 1860, the first 'Southern' station in the West End. It was designed by Robert Jacomb Hood and measured 800ft long and 230ft wide. The second part was opened two years later jointly by the London, Chatham & Dover Railway and the Great Western, and was served by mixed gauge tracks. Victoria enjoyed a large number of Pullman services and a couple of Pullmans are visible stabled in the sidings across from the carriage shed. Today it is the departure point for the luxury Venice Simplon-Orient Express as well as frequent fast services to Gatwick Airport. In the foreground of the view work is in progress on construction of the piers for Chelsea Bridge.   **B684**

Provincial Cities

Almost from the outset railways were regarded as inter-city transport. What had started as a means of moving heavy commodities like coal, slowly but in bulk, within industrial centres, quickly became a means of providing quick, efficient movement of goods and passengers between major centres. The Liverpool & Manchester Railway started it all, and the Great Western proved that railways were practical over long distances. Once the principle had been established, the major towns and cities were eager to be linked to their neighbours by rail.

For their part, the railway companies sought to display their confidence and to provide infrastructure of which everyone could be proud. As their systems became established, so their stations required enlargement and improvement. Some were rebuilt several times over, each new structure being finer and more commodious than the last.

In many instances the great boom in railway construction had led rival concerns to seek to serve the same places, so more often than not, provincial cities were left with a legacy of more than one major station. The Grouping of the railways in 1923 brought some of this rivalry to an end and put stations in a particular location under the control of the same company, but in other areas they were not brought together until Nationalisation. The Beeching Report of 1963 eliminated much duplication of routes and sought to centralise services on to one station wherever possible. In so doing, some fine structures were rendered redundant and sacrificed to the bulldozers. Twenty years on, the realisation has grown that 'rationalisation' was not always wise. Here and there, there are plans for the rails to return . . .

Cardiff, 1933

It is 1933 in Cardiff and an open-topped tram is crossing the River Taff on the Wood Street bridge adjacent to Cardiff General (now Central) station. The branch platforms serving the docks curve round to the right and beyond them can be seen the large water area of Bute Dock (see also the chapter on Docks). The Great Western undertook rebuilding at several major stations in the 1930s, introducing a distinctive tile-faced architecture which is still much in evidence, for instance at Bristol Temple Meads. Cardiff is here seen receiving the treatment with platforms and buildings in the midst of reconstruction. The view is looking eastwards, with down local and express trains at the platforms, the latter with a 'Castle' class 4-6-0 in charge. An up local is just departing and a branch train waits in the platform behind a rake of clerestory coaches awaiting their next duty. **41792**

Birmingham, 1933

Birmingham had two principal stations. The Great Western's
Snow Hill station was successively rebuilt and enlarged until
becoming a grand example of early 20th century work in
steel, glass and salt-faced red brick. Light and shadow played
through its roof in the style of New York's Grand Central.
New Street, well-placed for the city centre, was shared by
Midland and LNWR, becoming LMS at the Grouping, while
Snow Hill remained Great Western. Developed from small
beginnings, much of New Street was below ground level, with
sharply curving platforms. Like Snow Hill, it was reached
through tunnels, but presented an untidy and smoky
appearance. Its surroundings were totally redeveloped in the
postwar years, and New Street was rebuilt as part of the 25kV
electrification programme undertaken by London Midland
Region in the 1960s, whilst Snow Hill was closed. This fine
view shows New Street in 1933 before the blitz and
reconstruction altered the heart of the city. Trams and
Corporation buses may be seen in the streets around the
station. Today's New Street is one of the least satisfactory
1960s rebuilds: dirty, featureless concrete construction and
the very low roof adding to the feeling of being under
ground.   **41475**

Below:
The 11.30am Gloucester-Birmingham local train has just
arrived at Birmingham New Street, on 15 April 1958, headed
by '2P' class 4-4-0 No 40501. The sharply curved platform
arrangement can be seen. *M. Mensing*

Wolverhampton, 1946

Wolverhampton was also served by both the Great Western and the LNWR and was also reached by the Midland Railway. The ex-LNWR High Level station became LMS and was electrified as part of the 1960s scheme, while the GWR Low Level station suffered the same fate as Snow Hill and was closed. This interesting 1966 view took some detective work to caption, for Wolverhampton's railways are not too well covered in published histories. It shows the Great Western Railway's Stafford Road locomotive shed at the site of the Oxford, Worcester & Wolverhampton Railway's locomotive workshops. The line from the bottom left is the Herbert Street goods branch, which joins the mainline towards Wellington (Salop) at Stafford Road Junction. Part of Oxley Sidings is seen top right, and Dunstall Park station is adjacent to the motive power depot. At the bottom right an LMS express has just crossed the GWR main line and is hurrying towards High Level station. On shed may be seen a variety of small tank locomotives, while larger main line types are in steam on the far side of the buildings.   **A2444**

Bristol, 1954

Brunel was engineer to both the Great Western and the Bristol and Exeter Railways. At Bristol, they terminated close together but at right angles to one another. Through working was complicated, and during 1865-76 the present joint station was built to replace the other two. This fine view shows the severe curvature which was subtended by joining the two routes. Brunel's original Temple Meads station is off to the top left and was used until the mid-1960s by Midland line trains. Beyond it, in the top corner is part of the goods station. The tracks towards London curve away at the top, those at the bottom of the picture heading for Taunton and the west. St Philip's Marsh locomotive depot, its access controlled by an 'austerity' signalbox, is at the bottom right. The array of main line locomotives clearly show their BR livery. The station's finest feature is its clock-tower entrance with glazed steel canopies, seen top right, with immediately in front of it, the offices of the Bristol & Exeter Railway. Extensive restoration of the remaining historic structures, including the B&E office and the Brunel station, is in progress.   **R22269**

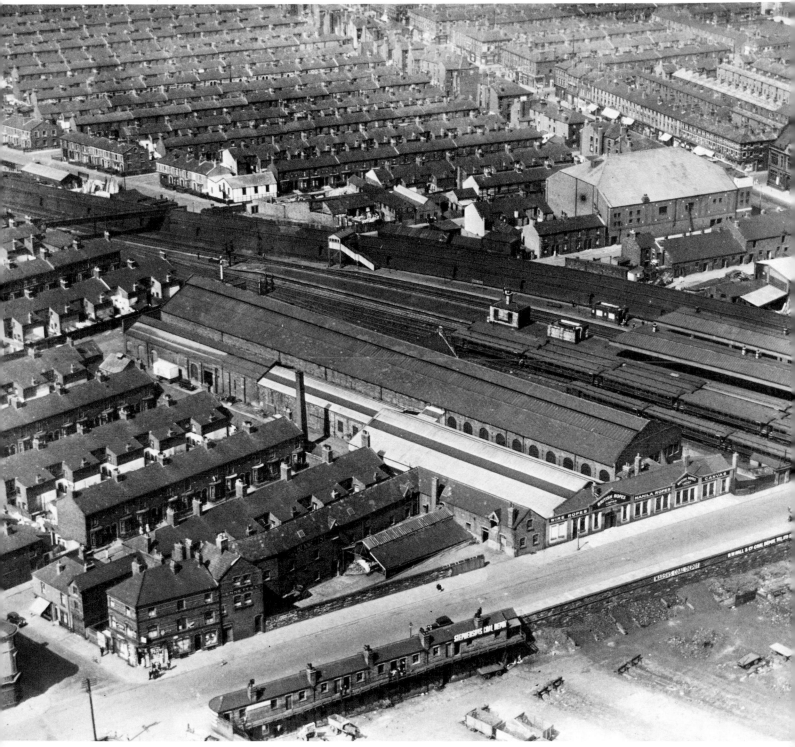

Liverpool, 1936

This is an example of the sort of picture which posed a real headache, because although I have been to Liverpool a couple of times, I cannot profess to any local knowledge, and certainly not of the scene 50 years ago. Captioned, 'Liverpool 1936', this is a view of the ex-Lancashire & Yorkshire Railway line out to Southport, which was electrified on the third rail system and is still so operated. A number of the ex-L&Y electric units, their clerestory roofs reminiscent of American 'interurban' trains, are stabled in the station. The electrified lines terminated at Liverpool Exchange station, but the location illustrated here is Bank Hall, one stop short of the terminus. Note the coal yard in the foreground, the British Ropes factory and the cinema just beyond the station.

Manchester, 1948

The Liverpool & Manchester Railway was, of course, the first trunk railway into the city of Manchester, but such was the city's importance that a number of rival railways sought access and left the city with four principal stations, Victoria, Exchange, Piccadilly and Central. The latter, grimy and blackened, is featured in this 1948 view. Central was the joint terminus of the Midland and the Cheshire Lines Committee, its Midland influence reflected in its similarity to St Pancras, at least in respect to the fine single-span roof. The city was an obvious candidate for rationalisation, and Manchester's main station is now Piccadilly, but only Central closed completely. After closure in 1969, it became a covered car park, falling into decay and dereliction, its future a source of continuing controversy. **A16000**

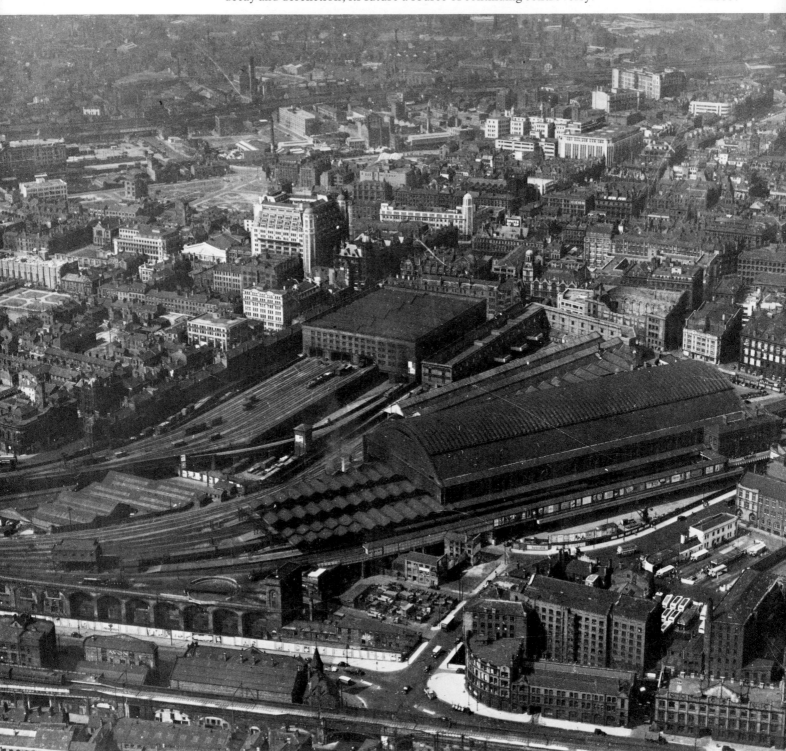

Glasgow, 1934

Glasgow Central High Level, seen here in 1934, is approached across the river Clyde, with fine road bridges either side. This view is looking towards the south bank of the river, with the station at the bottom left. This was the Caledonian Railway terminus of the West Coast route, via the LNWR, from London. Its adjoining Low Level station approaches it at right angles, just off the picture, and serves the lines out westwards to Dumbarton. One of the last big stations to be completed in the 19th century, it was a good example of urban development which benefited the local community and was one of the first stations to include offices and shops for letting. Several locomotives may be seen at work in the station and on the approaches, and the top of one of the graceful Clyde steamers can be seen in the foreground. Beyond the river the Glasgow & Paisley Joint line, (Caledonian and Glasgow & South Western) diverges to the right.   **48777**

Newcastle, 1924

Two tank locomotives are seen marshalling stock at the
eastern end of Newcastle Central station in 1924. Originated
by the Newcastle & Carlisle Railway, the station became part
of the extensive North Eastern Railway system. Some local
services were electrified, although this isolated electric
system was abandoned in the 1960s, more recently to be
replaced by the Tyne & Wear rapid transit system. The main
line to the north leaves the picture on the right, while the
Gateshead line curves sharply to the south to cross the river
Tyne. The complex and heavily used crossing of tracks seen
in the centre was replaced by British Railways in 1949, using
manganese steel rail sections in order to withstand the
exceptional wear. Note the open-topped tram in the street
below the 'Y' of the junction.   **10344**

Left:
A view, from the castle, of the down 'Fying Scotsman'
passing non-stop through Newcastle on 28 July 1948. The
locomotive is Gresley 'A4' 4-6-2 No 60012 *Commonwealth of
Australia*, carrying the early British Railways light blue
livery. The service had been restored to its prewar schedule
only a few weeks earlier. *K. C. Footer*

Edinburgh, 1954

The Caledonian Railway's terminus in Edinburgh was at Princes Street, seen here in 1954.
The principal Edinburgh station, Waverley, was ex-North British Railway, and is just visible
at the top right. The tracks west from Waverley plunge into a tunnel (centre) to pass under
the Caledonian's Lothian Street goods depot. Princes Street, the city's stylish shopping street,
runs diagonally across the top of the picture, with its well-known monument visible top right.
Here, again, was an opportunity for rationalisation, and in 1965 services were concentrated
on Waverley, and the Princes Street terminus was closed.   **R21180**

Hull, 1950

The fine terminal station at Hull Paragon in 1950, with some bomb damage to surrounding structures (right), still evident. Anlaby Road passes diagonally in front of the station and the booking office with its imposing entrance columns can be seen. Inside the station are numerous rakes of Gresley LNER coaches, most still in their original teak, or wartime brown livery. There is an abundance of ex-NER 4-6-2T locomotives in evidence. Beyond the station lies the bus station and bus garage. Despite the declining fortunes of its staple fishing industry, Hull remains an important centre and now has a service of IC125 trains to London. **A28629**

Leeds, 1926

The very complex railway scene at Leeds in 1926, where the LNER and LMS had acquired facilities bequeathed by the Great Northern, North Eastern, Midland, and London & North Western Railways. From the left in this picture are Wellington Street goods depot (GN, NER, Midland), Leeds Central passenger station (NER), the River Aire, Leeds Wellington passenger station (Midland) and Leeds New passenger station (NER). The Leeds and Liverpool Canal cuts through the foreground. The two stations at the right form the site of the present Leeds City station. Tracks in the foreground diverge left towards Armley and right towards Hunslet, and a clerestory-roofed local train can be seen coming off the Armley line. Here, again, rationalisation was inevitable and a completely new station resulted, Leeds Central being closed in April 1967. **P15705**

Major Depots and Workshops

As the major railway companies concentrated their heavy engineering activities in particular centres, they had the effect either of creating 'railway towns' or of taking over as the town's principal employer. More than any other section in the book, this chapter warrants a representative view from each of the 'Big Four' railway companies, but that cannot be. Derby was a notable omission from the available prints, while the Southern Railway's centre at Eastleigh was also missed.

Such has been the contraction of the railway industry in postwar years that a number of these great railway centres are just a pale shadow of their former selves, or in some cases have been wiped out completely as far as railway engineering activity is concerned.

It seems likely that Derby, the railway town established by the Midland Railway, will eventually become the only survivor where railway engineering remains a major employer — scarcely imaginable when one considers the scale of operations at some of the other sites.

Leicester, 1948

Leicester London Road (LMS) station in 1948 looking south. The station is top left with the LMS goods and grain warehouse boldly proclaiming itself, extreme right. Next to it is a large covered freight shed, and the centre-piece is the modern roundhouse, with a 2-6-4T being turned on the central turntable. At left is the water tank and a second turntable. Ash pits and modest coaling facilities are visible beyond the roundhouse and a number of loaded coal wagons are present. The signalbox controlling the area is visible to the right of the roundhouse, with departmental vehicles stabled alongside. **A16188**

Swindon, 1954

A postwar view of Swindon, GWR, the most recent railway town to lose its railway workshops in the name of progress. Indeed, as this was being written, the final section of the works site was sold for more than £9 million. However, the area shown in this view was gradually whittled away from the 1960s onwards, and almost the entire area is now occupied by insurance offices and 'high-tech' industry. At right, from top to bottom runs the London-Bristol main line, with the Gloucester line diverging and a six-coach local train from Gloucester approaching Swindon Junction station. All the carriage workshops to the right of the main line, and even the right-hand platforms of the station, have been gone for some 15 years. In the left and centre are the carriage and wagon workshops, the machine shop, stores and locomotive shed, all now gone. Below the Gloucester line are the offices, smiths and an erecting shop, most of which closed in 1986.   **A53783**

Below:
A view inside the main erecting shop at Swindon works — simply known as 'A Shop' — on 22 April 1927. A large number of locomotives are under repair, and on the left 'Star' 4-6-0 No 4022 *King William* (subsequently renamed *The Belgian Monarch*) is suspended from the overhead gantry hoist. *Ian Allan Library*

Swindon, 1924

For some 40 years up to the Grouping in 1923, the Great Western did not have Swindon to itself. Encouraged by the Midland and the LSWR, the Midland & South Western Junction Railway bisected GWR territory with its Cheltenham-Andover route and had its principle station and head office in Swindon. This is Swindon Town station in 1924, only a year after the MSWJR had been swallowed up by its big rival. A local to Swindon Junction, headed by an MSWJR 0-6-0T stands at the three-platform station, which boasted its own refreshment room. The goods shed can be seen below and to the right. At left, above the station, the fine house with the three gables was the MSWJR office. The line closed completely in 1961, although freight to Swindon Town lasted a few more years. **10118**

Doncaster, 1953

The Great Northern Railway established Doncaster as a railway town and it subsequently became the main locomotive works of the LNER. Many famous locomotives were turned out from the workshops in this picture, including Gresley's *Flying Scotsman* and the speed record-holder *Mallard*. Known as 'The Plant', Doncaster works stands close by the station, as seen in this view on 21 April 1953. A down freight is making leisurely progress through the station, as another emerges from the sidings. Stock for a local passenger service is being readied behind the South signalbox. Note the footbridge across the station to give access to the works, and the number of vehicles awaiting attention in the works yard.   **R18312**

York, 1961

A priceless view of the heart of the railway system at York. BR Mk 1 Travelling Post Office stock is visible at bottom right, where one can see how the railway has been kept outside the city wall, a corner of which is seen at bottom right. Immediately opposite is the mighty curved roof of York station. At right, above the station, is the locomotive depot, which is nowadays the National Railway Museum, and to its left with the gleaming 'white' roof is the goods depot which now forms the Museum's Peter Allen annexe. To the left of this, in the centre of the picture is York wagon works, now just a minor repair depot. The lines converge at Poppleton Junction beyond the wagon works, and the branch to Poppleton and Knaresborough diverges to the left. The large group of buildings on the left are the former NER carriage works, nowadays BREL York, which is still a major multiple-unit carriage builder for BR. Note, east of the station, the two former roundhouses, one with its roof off but still with turntable and tracks inside.

A91490

Crewe, 1953

Ironically, not much of the workshops area is shown in this view of the town which is probably the most synonymous with railway works. This view of Crewe does provide a marvellous view of the station, and particularly its roof detail which mixes modest train sheds with extensive ridge-and-furrow canopies. Top left can be seen a corner of the works area, and part of the locomotive shed. The three diverging lines serve, from left to right, Chester and North Wales, Carlisle and Glasgow, and Manchester, while the converging lines at the bottom are respectively from Shrewsbury and Stafford   **19271**

Thornaby, 1962

An ex-War Department 2-8-0 runs light past the octagonal roundhouse at Thornaby-on-Tees in 1962. When built, this was the country's most modern roundhouse, but by this time it had been superseded by a large, modern diesel depot and some of its complement of Derby and Birmingham RC&W Type 2 locomotives can be seen on the right. Beyond the diesel depot, the remaining steam allocation is concentrated on a small rectangular shed, and a 'J94' 0-6-0ST, a 'B1' 4-6-0, another 'WD' and numerous 0-6-0s are present, although few are in steam. The river Tees may be seen in the background, the surrounding industries of steelworks and chemical plants providing the kind of traffic for which the depot's motive power has been carefully selected.   **A98447**

Toton, 1948

This bird's eye view of Toton shed looks like a model with the roof lifted off to show what is inside. Grouped around the central turntable in the style of a roundhouse, are LMS '8F' 2-8-0s and '5MT' 4-6-0s, plus a couple of 'Jinty' 0-6-0Ts and a solitary diesel shunter. By far the largest locomotives are the least conspicuous. Tucked in parallel to the nearer wall are two of the mighty Beyer-Garratt 2-6-0+0-6-2Ts. These locomotives, on their regular Toton-Brent coal train duties, feature in at least two other illustrations elsewhere in this book.   **A16189**

Bridges

The railway engineers, great and small, left us a
legacy of fine bridges, many of which still survive and
carry far heavier traffic than that for which they were
intended. Not all were grand structures forming
imposing links in a vital transport chain, such as the
Royal Border Bridge at Berwick and the Royal
Albert Bridge at Saltash. Some, such as Brunel's
effort at Saltash and Stephenson's across the Menai
Strait used novel techniques to overcome particular
problems. Others were simply a means to an end, to
cross a valley or to take the railway over a river or
estuary without a lengthy and expensive detour.

Ouse Viaduct, 1949
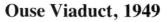

The London, Brighton & South Coast Railway's Ouse
Viaduct at Haywards Heath, Sussex, on the main line to
Brighton ranks 12th in the list of Britain's longest bridges. It
is 1,420ft long, and at 92ft high, is also one of the highest.
Dating from 1840, it was designed by J. U. Rastrick with
balustrades and architectural embellishments by David
Mocatta, who was responsible for much of the fine
architecture on the LBSCR. The 37 spans, each of 30ft, carry
two tracks, but now see considerably more and heavier traffic
than was originally envisaged. In this view, a 4-LAV electric
multiple-unit is crossing the viaduct on a local service. **A22733**

Leslie Viaduct, 1932

1932 view of Leslie, a small town in Fife, served by the ex-North British Railway branch line from Markinch and closed to passengers as long ago as January 1932. A fine masonry viaduct of 14 arches spans the valley to bring the line to its terminus at Leslie. Such delicate and attractive structures were typical of the builders of many of Britain's railways, and though many were destroyed when lines were closed, they left us with a priceless architectural heritage.

40413

St Pinnock Viaduct, 1948

A GWR 'Hall' class 4-6-0 heads a local train, with milk tanks on the rear, over St Pinnock Viaduct near Bodmin Road station. Brunel made use of Cornwall's plentiful, inexpensive timber for many of the viaducts on the Cornwall Railway. His distinctive wooden spans comprised a series of individual frames, spread like a fan from each of the supporting masonry piers. Like all wooden bridges, they required constant maintenance, and towards the end of the 19th century a programme of replacement was begun. New viaducts were built beside the old, or in some instances as here, the masonry piers were built up and the spans replaced with lattice girders. The last of its kind, Penryn on the Falmouth branch was replaced in 1932.

A14990

Royal Border Bridge, 1949

A panoramic view of the Royal Border Bridge at Berwick upon Tweed, looking northwards, with Berwick on the far bank of the river. In the foreground is Tweedmouth, with its modest station dwarfed by the goods yard and substantial locomotive depot. Steam can be seen coming from a number of locomotives at Tweedmouth and also down the main line beyond Berwick station. Old and new road bridges are visible in the centre, downstream of the railway viaduct. Note too, the 'cut' from the river which has enabled a small coaster to enter the pool beside the oil storage tanks. This is a 1949 view.

A22833

Severn Bridge, 1949

The Severn and Wye Joint Railway crossed the Severn estuary by means of the Severn Bridge; at 4,161ft Britain's third longest railway bridge. This view, taken on 2 March 1949, shows the bridge from the Monmouthshire shore with Severn Bridge station on the curve in the foreground, and looking towards the Gloucester shore. The S&WJ was jointly operated by the Great Western and Midland Railways, though most of the structures were of Midland appearance. The Severn Bridge was single track throughout and able to accommodate only the lightest locomotives. **C18739**

Severn Bridge, 1963

The Severn Bridge comprised 21 wrought iron bow string girder spans plus a lifting section over the Gloucester & Berkeley Canal. The largest spans were two totalling 327ft to allow navigation by the largest vessels requiring access to the upper estuary. On a foggy night in 1960 a barge running out of control took out one of these spans completely. The Bridge was not repaired and stood for a number of years in its severed state before eventually being dismantled by contractors. **A117657**

Wakefield, 1935

Captioned simply as a prewar view of Wakefield, this photograph apparently shows Westgate Junction looking south down the West Riding & Grimsby Joint line with the L&Y Normanton-Crigglestone route crossing from left to right near the top of the picture. North of Westgate, the line is of GN origin and at left a curve leads down to connect with the L&Y towards Normanton. Of particular interest in this picture is the volume of bridgework, over 100 masonry arches, yet forming a structure which is not particularly remarkable in British railway civil engineering because in towns and cities, large and small, there were many such structures which were the means by which the early railway engineers managed to pick their way through densely built-up areas or across low-lying or waterlogged ground. Today, many such viaducts still carry heavy traffic, while their arches have become a saleable commodity as small ready-made industrial premises. **48497**

Conway, 1961

A wealth of noble British architecture and bridge engineering is shown in this view of Conway, taken on 9 July 1961. Grand medieval fortifications abound along the Welsh coast but few are more imposing than Conway, sited overlooking the river estuary. Faced with building his railway along the North Wales coast so close to such an important monument, Stephenson produced a bridge to match, with fine castellated portals through which trains entered the spans. The latter were built as square tubes, obtaining their strength from the 'box-girder' shape, with the trains running through the middle. The much larger and more spectacular Britannia Tubular Bridge across the Menai Strait to Anglesey was a development of the Conway design. Note also, the pedestrian suspension bridges and the modern road bridge. **A93909**

Royal Albert Bridge, 1939

Isambard Kingdom Brunel's last great railway work was the Royal Albert Bridge over the River Tamar at Saltash. The Admiralty insisted on a headroom of 100ft and no more than one mid-stream pier and Brunel's design featured suspension chains from eliptical tubes which themselves carried some of the weight. The two main trusses, each 445ft long, were assembled on the shore, floated out and gradually jacked into place. Brunel supervised the positioning of the first span in 1857 and the band played 'See, the Conquering Hero Cometh', but by the time the second span was ready he was too ill to take part. The bridge was opened by the Prince Consort in 1859 and Brunel died only four months later. Over the years various parts of the bridge have been replaced or strengthened without affecting the appearance of the bridge. This beautiful vista, on 14 August 1939, when the bridge was 80 years old, was ruined in the 1960s by construction of the overpowering road bridge which is visually both too large and too close to the Brunel bridge. In the foreground may be seen the chain-operated vehicle ferry or floating bridge which was the means by which road vehicles were obliged to cross the river at this point, prior to construction of the road bridge. A lengthy detour inland was the only alternative. **R6568**

Right:
The portals of the Royal Albert Bridge, Saltash, were inscribed as a memorial to their designer, who died shortly after the bridge was completed in 1859. *British Railways*

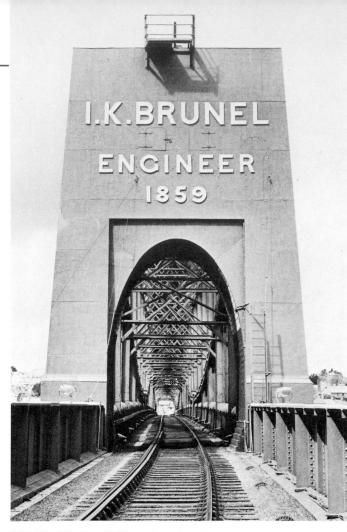

Tay Bridge, 1947

A bridge which met a sticky end was the North British Railway's first crossing of the Firth of Tay, which collapsed into the river during a gale on 28 December 1879. The new lattice girder structure was sited 60ft upstream of the old, and is a solidly built and unattractive structure. In this 1947 view, the piers of the old bridge can be seen, and a lengthy freight train is crossing the bridge from the Dundee side. The Tay Bridge has a total of 85 spans and measures 10,711ft overall. It carries two tracks, 83ft 6in above high water and is built of wrought iron and brick. It was opened on 20 June 1887. **A5299**

On the River

Prior to the development of the railway system, the only really practical way to transport heavy or bulky commodities over any great distance was by water. The 18th century saw growth in coastal shipping and the major development of navigable inland waterways through the construction of canals and the development of locks to control the rivers and produce navigable channels. The superior speed and convenience of railways rapidly wiped out much of this waterway development but the competition between the two modes often led to rail routes following closely the navigable waterways and having interchange facilities.

The photographs in this section show the railway cheek-by-jowl with the river. In one or two instances both are closely serving industry, in others the railway is providing access to a popular riverside resort, or simply following the river valley as the easiest route for construction. Surprisingly, even in the industrial context the river valleys provide attractive scenery to be viewed through the carriage window, while from our unique aerial viewpoint we can argue that the presence of the railway actually adds something to, rather than detracts from the beauty of the scene.

Pangbourne, 1955

Brunel's choice of route for the original Great Western main line from London to Bristol clings to the Thames Valley from its first crossing of the river at Maidenhead to near Didcot. It is almost level, with sweeping curves, and is consequently very fast, allowing today's 125mph InterCity expresses to exploit their full potential. Here, the main line is seen at Pangbourne, west of Reading, one of the closest stations to the River Thames, its forecourt opening on to the river bank. Reading is to the right and the line at this point has four tracks. The fast lines are nearest the camera, with the up and down relief lines (the Great Western never called them 'slow' lines!) nearest the river. Pangbourne's four-platform red brick station in standard GWR style was typical of those built after the broad gauge conversion and when the line was quadrupled. In recent years it has suffered rationalisation with the loss of the goods shed and yard (extreme left) and removal of the down fast platform since no trains routed over the fast line are booked to stop. The urban sprawl of Reading has enveloped Pangbourne since this 12 May 1955 view, and the moorings along this stretch of the river are today jammed with pleasure boats. **R23245**

Bude, 1932

The railway did not reach the Cornish resort and harbour at Bude until the comparatively late date of 1898. The Bude and Holsworthy Canal was navigable for only about 1½ of its original 30 miles by the time this 1932 photograph of Bude was taken. For much of its distance the Halwill Junction-Bude branch paralleled the rivers Bude and Strat, the latter visible in the centre. Bude station was on the edge of the town and this view shows the goods lines which extended beyond the station to the harbour, formed as a basin on the B&H Canal. Standard gauge wagons are visible on the quay. There was extensive traffic in sand from Bude, originally served by a primitive flangeway from the beach which enabled sand to be tipped into barges or railway wagons for onward transport. In the 1920s the flangeway was replaced by a narrow gauge contractors railway with trains of side-tipping wagons which are visible on the wharf. A popular resort, served by the 'Atlantic Coast Express' from Waterloo, Bude boasted Men's (18-hole) and Ladies (9-hole) golf courses, visible in the background of this view of the area known as Bude Haven. The branch line from Halwill Junction was axed under Beeching in October 1966. **C18012**

Balloch, 1961

The beautiful Loch Lomond provides a major recreational area close to the conurbations of Glasgow and pleasure boats plied its waters as early as 1817. The Dumbarton & Balloch Railway provided a vital 8½-mile link from the Firth of Forth across to the Loch, its rails terminating at Balloch Pier. It was served by constituents of both the LMS and LNER and when these companies jointly acquired the Loch steamer services, the little D&B became jointly managed. This view, in 1961 shows Balloch Pier with a steamer moored and a host of small pleasure craft on the Loch. In the distance is Balloch Town station with its goods yard and carriage sidings, plus a disused turntable. A solitary siding serves the slipway adjacent to the pier, where the Loch steamers are dry-docked during the off-season. Masts and catenary are in place for the commencement of Glasgow suburban 'Blue Train' electrification, but the work is apparently incomplete and locomotive-hauled stock still occupies the platform and sidings. **A88148**

Windsor, 1926

Here are two splendid historic views of one of England's most historic towns, Windsor, which is also the author's home town. Essentially a resort town, Windsor has been dominated by the Castle since the time of William the Conqueror, who found this small hill overlooking a great bend in the River Thames an ideal spot for fortification. The river sweeps to the left through this view, then swings right to cross the top of the picture. On the left bank is Eton, with the College Boat Club's skiffs much in evidence, while steamers and pleasure boats are moored on the opposite bank. Beyond Eton Bridge, the wide sweeping train shed of William Tite's LSWR Windsor & Eton Riverside station can be seen. This fine roof was demolished circa 1960. At right, adjacent to the gas works, is the GWR Windsor & Eton Central station built in 1897 for Queen Victoria's Diamond Jubilee. The whitish-coloured train shed covers the Royal station which now houses Madame Tussaud's 'Royalty and Empire' exhibition. The station itself now has but a single track and platform, the goods yard having become a coach park. The date of this view is 1926. A train of four- and six-wheel coaches stands in Platform 1 and a long excursion train in Platform 3, while a Pannier tank takes water at the end of Platform 4. A 'Metro' 2-4-0T is heading out over the arches with a five-coach branch train to Slough. **C18678 (1599)**

Windsor, 1921

Five years earlier, in 1921, the Aerofilms photographer swooped low over Windsor to capture this interesting view of the weir and the 'cut' leading to Romney Lock. A pleasure boat and rowing boat make leisurely progress upstream on a stretch of the Thames which nowadays bustles with boating activity. To the right is the LSWR branch from Staines and the station throat of Windsor & Eton Riverside with Home Park, the venue for the annual Royal Windsor Horse Show, top right. An 'M7' 0-4-4T runs back over the up line before entering the sidings to be turned and coaled ready for its next turn of duty. It is passing the signalbox and immediately beyond it a scissors crossover can be seen. The carriage sidings are well filled and a small crane stands at the end of an isolated track length along the wharf edge, in readiness for any goods requiring transhipment from the river. The line to Windsor Riverside was electrified on the third-rail 660V dc system in the 1930s, and today only passenger trains, Royal trains and summer excursions use the line. Riverside development has engulfed the yard and cars park where the carriage sidings were once situated. **6296**

Henley, 1928

Another Thames-side resort served by the Great Western Railway is Henley, seen here in 1928. The town is famous for its annual regatta, and at the time of this photograph its pleasing red brick Georgian character had not been too badly impacted by modern development. A railway to the town was first proposed in 1846 but it was 1857 before the short branch from Twyford was constructed. The substantial terminus dominates this view with the turntable on the right and the goods yard in the foreground. The station and goods shed were built to accommodate broad gauge track and display distinctly Brunelian styling. The Henley branch was reduced to single track around 1960 and subsequently the line and its terminus have been periodically rationalised, until at Henley, only a truncated length of one platform now remains, the original buildings having all gone. **C17429**

Chepstow, 1921

It is hard now to imagine that ship building on this scale once took place on the River Wye, yet this 25 March 1921 view of Chepstow shows two coasters under construction, with keels being laid for four more. All the slipways are rail-served for the delivery of materials, while a large rail-served warehouse is being constructed on adjacent land. The station itself, with fine Brunelian chalet buildings, can be seen on the left with the main line towards Gloucester sweeping round to cross the river by the distinctive tubular suspension bridge. The curious bridge design was necessary in order to comply with requirements for a minimum headroom at high water, and the much larger Royal Albert Bridge, Saltash followed the same design principle for similar reasons. By 1960 large ships had ceased to navigate the River Wye and the bridge was rebuilt, with the present structure carried on the original piers. **C15742**

Above left:
Brunel's Chepstow bridge, seen from the cab of a Swansea-Birmingham diesel train. *Andrew F. Smith*

Left:
The end of tall-masted sailing ships meant that it was no longer necessary to maintain a great headroom under the Chepstow bridge. Thus, the replacement span, seen here in 1962 when new, could employ an underslung girder arrangement. *British Railways*

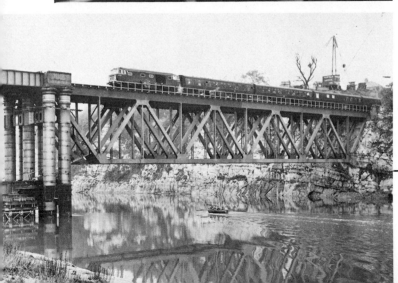

Ironbridge, 1934

Two views are included here, of Ironbridge Gorge in the Severn Valley, known as 'the cradle of the industrial revolution'. It was close to here that Abraham Darby developed his smelting process and the centrepiece of the scene is the world's first iron bridge, dating from 1770 and cast in Darby's local Coalbrookdale ironworks. In the first view, right by the end of the bridge, we see Ironbridge station on the Shrewsbury-Hartlebury 'Severn Valley' line. Beyond the station a private quarry siding is visible, and in the far distance the fine Albert Bridge carries the Wellington-Craven Arms line over the Severn, to cross the Severn Valley line at Buildwas Junction. Ironbridge yard is well filled and the town is busy in this 1934 view.   **46398**

Ironbridge, 1949

The second view is some 15 years more recent, evidenced by the appearance of the Midland Red single-deck bus turning on the bridge approach opposite 'The Tontine' hotel. By this time the bridge had been restricted to pedestrian use only, and the large white block of shops to the left of the bridge approach had been demolished. The station is seen more clearly, its attractive yellow brick building being one of few on the Severn Valley line without adjoining living accommodation. There is a black timber goods shed, a level crossing and standard GWR signalbox, and the rather unusual provision, for this line, of a footbridge. A '2251' class 0-6-0 is shunting its train of open wagons into the sidings. The Severn Valley line closed in 1962 and this section was lifted soon afterwards. The station quickly became derelict and was demolished after the chimney stack collapsed through the roof. The site is now a car park.   **A24217**

Major Rail Yards

The marshalling yard was for many years a central feature of railway freight operations. With thousands of daily movements of individual vehicles or small groups of wagons to and from a multitude of different destinations it was vital to have well thought out yards with sufficient capacity to enable speedy re-marshalling of freight trains. These were places where trains were simply broken down and remade. If loading or unloading facilities were provided, these would be in a separate area of sidings.

Some marshalling yards were provided with a hump from which wagons could run under their own momentum into sorting sidings. Others simply employed shunting locomotives to move the vehicles. Defective wagons would be removed to 'cripple' sidings, and there would be storage roads for brake vans.

New yards were still being developed into the early 1960s, but the elimination of the so-called 'wagon-load' freight operations and the concentration of freight into block trains of a single commodity for a single destination has reduced the need for re-marshalling, and one by one the big yards have either closed or been rationalised to a fraction of their former size. Those which remain serve mainly the Speedlink service and engineering department use.

Cricklewood, 1955

At the London end of the Midland main line lies Cricklewood, seen here in 1955. The marshalling yard is a comparatively modest affair, top left, with the twin rectangular 'roundhouses' of the locomotive depot visible in the distance beyond it. The station is in the foreground and to its right with the white roof, is the dairy depot, with milk tanks on the adjacent siding. Beyond it is the express goods depot for van-load traffic, while general merchandise is handled in the crowded yard on the other side of the line.   **A59184**

Ripple Lane, 1957

The British Railways Modernisation Plan accepted that the frequent re-marshalling of trains slowed their overall progress and sought to concentrate the activities of many smaller yards into a number of major marshalling yards at strategic locations. One of a number of yards which was redeveloped in line with this philosophy was Ripple Lane at Barking, Essex, seen here in 1957. Recent work at the nearer end shows up the control building and contrasts the black areas of the retarders which slowed the wagons down, with the white of newly-ballasted track. To the left of this area, the pale grey tops of five of the then new Brush Type 2 (later Class 31) diesels can be seen. So severe were the changes in freight traffic operations proposed in the Beeching Report of 1963 that Ripple Lane was considered for closure as its main purpose would have gone. However, much of the yard area remains in use today by trains to and from the industrial areas of the north bank of the Thames. **A94788**

Millerhill, 1960

The Scottish Region of British Railways inherited a formidable number, some 80 in all, of small yards, many of which were badly placed or duplicated each other's functions. By the late 1950s the Region had embarked on a scheme to replace more than 40 of them with five new yards, and here we see one of them under construction. The site is at Monktonhall, southeast of Edinburgh, where the new Millerhill yard is under construction, in 1960. The main line in the centre is a freight-only route, and on either side of it land has been cleared and infilled. The huge fans of pointwork and sidings have been laid from one end and the site clearance work plainly shows the eventual shape of the unfinished ends. This is the view looking northwards. **R38407**

Toton, 1951

Toton motive power depot features elsewhere in this book, but here we see the entire Toton set-up, with the locomotive depot just a small part of a vast operation. The staple traffic here is coal, and in this postwar view the main line runs from bottom left, up through the centre of the picture. The view is looking north, with Stapleford & Sandiacre station in the distance. To the left the yard deals mainly with returning empty wagons, and beyond is the locomotive depot with its concrete coaling tower clearly visible. At the time of this view, the shed still had its roof. To the right of the line, the yard has its own separate white control tower, and diesel shunters and '4F' 0-6-0s are at work among the trains of loaded wagons. In the foreground is the wagon repair works which would deal with running repairs to defective wagons. **R15974**

Crewe, 1954

A grandstand view of the marshalling yard at Crewe in 1954 showing the assortment of general merchandise traffic, as opposed to concentration on a particular commodity such as at Toton. At the top left can be seen part of the goods shed and also the locomotive depot. The coaling tower and turntable can be seen and a variety of steam locomotives are in evidence. Nevertheless, what appears to be white-coloured catenary masts are visible in the background, while an electrification wiring train is stabled near the MPD. A mixture of steam and diesel shunters are at work in the yard which is strategically placed at the junction of a number of routes so as to break down and reform trains for destinations all over Northwest England and Western Scotland, as well as North Wales. **A53946**

Millerhill, 1972

Another view of Millerhill Yard, this time looking southwards. Working from the bottom right we see the stabling area for brake vans. At top right, merry-go-round coal hoppers stand outside a small depot. In the main yard are numerous empty coal wagons, together with a number of bulk grain vehicles operating in connection with the Scotch whisky industry. In the middle sidings are rakes of coaching stock mainly comprising the Swindon-built Class 126 Inter-City diesel units, presumably en route to or from works. Beyond these are bogie wagons loaded with new concrete-sleepered track sections, and near the back, perhaps the most interesting detail of all — no fewer than 15 of the Clayton Class 17 diesel locomotives. These were at one time intended as the standard Type 1 design but proved unreliable, and those seen here are withdrawn and await scrapping.   **A222923**

New Works

One of the principal reasons for aerial photography is that it provides a unique means of showing the scale and impact upon the landscape of major construction works. Nowadays designers and planners are more attuned to the need for assessing the impact of their efforts on our crowded environment. It was not always so, and consequently the Aerofilms selection of prints showing new railway works tends to be concentrated on postwar developments, most other major railway developments having taken place prior to the origin of these aerial surveys which began in the 1920s.

The accompanying views do, however, give us an unusual view of one or two important railway developments. In some cases they involve comparisons of two illustrations from different dates, so strict observance of chronological order has not been possible.

Bletchley, 1938

Here we have two fine views of the ex-LNWR main line at Bletchley, an important railway 'crossroads' which now forms part of the Milton Keynes conurbation. Taken in 1938, the first view shows the eight-platform station with its tremendously complex track layout controlled by large LNWR signalboxes at both ends. Top right, the line from Oxford converges with the main line from London, while bottom left, the route to Bedford diverges. Oxford-Cambridge line trains thus had to cross the entire layout at Bletchley and many of these were freights which had no reason actually to call at Bletchley. The result was a considerable bottleneck. At bottom centre is Bletchley motive power depot with a LNWR 0-8-0 coming off the turntable, as an up freight approaches on the main line. **56948**

Bletchley, 1960

A view of Bletchley from the opposite direction. The main line from London enters the picture at bottom right and the Oxford line bottom left. The main line crosses the picture diagonally, and the route to Bedford and Cambridge can be seen heading away through extensive yards towards Fenny Stratford at top right. In the centre the Bletchley flyover is under construction, its purpose in carrying Oxford-Cambridge line trains over and around the station being quite plain from this view. Hailed as one of the features of 'Britain's new railway' of the early 1960s, its usefulness was quickly eroded by falling traffic levels on this route. The station has also been modernised with new lamps, a footbridge with goods lift towers and a new locomotive shed.   **38033**

Potters Bar, 1951

Potters Bar station in Hertfordshire, seen in 1951, before work commenced on the quadrupling of tracks on the former Great Northern outer suburban section. Note the four station houses in matching style to the yellow brick station building. The small but busy goods yard has extensive coal distribution staithes; an aspect of local railway services which has virtually disappeared thanks to smokeless zones and central heating. The station was completely rebuilt as part of the quadrupling scheme, and new concrete platforms carry modern concrete and glass structures. It was further transformed with the installation of overhead 25kV electrification some 20 years later. **A41496**

Hadley Wood, 1959

Next station up the line from Potters Bar is Hadley Wood, and here the quadrupling involved boring new tunnels on either side of the station. This view, actually captioned as 'Potters Bar', shows Hadley Wood, with the new station served from the original booking hall on the overbridge, and with the new North Tunnel portal clearly visible beyond the station. The extent of earthworks is readily apparent with the shallow new slopes to the cutting sides. A rake of Cravens diesel multiple-units makes gingerly progress down the new slow line, but the new up line is obliterated by ballast and is still being worked on.   A74916

Right:
Hadley Wood North tunnels with the new tracks on the left. In the late evening of 31 May 1963, Class A4 4-6-2 No 60021 *Wild Swan*, a sister to the record-breaking *Mallard* is hurrying an up express towards King's Cross.
Brian Haresnape

Calstock

All that is best about the English landscape is exemplified in this view of Calstock, situated on the Cornish bank of the River Tamar. The first railway into the village was an isolated industrial line, the East Cornwall Minerals Railway, whose prime purpose was to transport coal from Calstock Quay to mining operations in the surrounding countryside. Coal was required to power the mining engines and pumps and the only economical way to bring it in was by sea and up the Tamar to Calstock. To reach the quay from railway track level, a rope-worked incline with a stationary winding engine was provided.

In the final years of the 19th century plans were made to link Calstock with the LSWR main line at Bere Alston and the famous light railway operator, Colonel Holman F. Stephens was enlisted as engineer. The line was completed in 1907, the major engineering feature being the viaduct over the Tamar at Calstock. Its 12 arches were each 60ft span and 120ft high and it was built of concrete blocks. A wagon lift capable of carrying one loaded coal wagon of 15 tons weight was installed by the third arch on the Calstock side and replaced the incline to the quay. The railway was extended, over part of the old ECMR route, to Callington and eventually passed into the ownership of the Southern Railway and later BR.

The SR main line through Bere Alston was closed under Beeching, and the Callington branch was also proposed for closure. However there are no road crossings of the Tamar at this point, and only the Saltash bridge south of Calstock, so it was felt desirable to maintain the rail link in to Plymouth. The section beyond Gunnislake, to Callington was closed, however. Regular service trains still cross Calstock viaduct and serve the village, but the pretty little light railway station building, of typical H. F. Stephens style seen in this picture, has since been removed. BR's new 'Skipper' diesel railcars proved unsatisfactory on the sharp curves and steep inclines of the branch (note the curves on the left) and conventional diesel units have had to be retained for the time being. **AC294733**

Gatwick, 1953

In less than 35 years this scene has been transformed beyond recognition. The four-track London-Brighton main line now carries an intensive service of trains to serve this, London's 'second' airport, at Gatwick in Surrey. This was the scene on 15 July 1953 with the old Gatwick station serving the aerodrome, at which wartime fighter planes are being dismantled. At left are a number of Spitfires and Seafires, together with dismembered fuselages and racks containing wings. At right, a Dragon Rapide and two Oxfords are the only physical evidence of Gatwick's impending role as a major passenger airport. It is not, despite its popular image, just a 'package holiday' airport. The author has twice flown to Vancouver direct from Gatwick, having arrived by the fast, frequent and impressive electric train service to the new station. **A50735**

Woodhead, 1952

Another major tunnelling project of the 1950s was the construction of the new Woodhead Tunnel on the former GCR Manchester-Sheffield route. The tunnel was necessary in order to obtain sufficient clearance for overhead electrification on the 1,500V dc system, under a scheme conceived by the LNER before Nationalisation. The tunnel took the line under the Pennines at its summit and was 3 miles 66yd long. It opened to traffic in 1954. Despite its youth and modernity, the tunnel had a brief service life. By the 1970s, the prewar electrification system was outdated and in need of renewal. There was insufficient remaining trans-Pennine traffic to justify repair or replacement, so the Woodhead Route closed and the track was lifted, leaving much older tunnels on other routes to carry the freight traffic between Sheffield and Manchester. **A43357**

Swindon

This view of Swindon works in the early 1970s makes an interesting comparison with the earlier views elsewhere in this book. The camera is looking towards the west, with Swindon station just off the bottom right hand corner. The Gloucester line curves away to the right and Brunel's route to Bristol passes along the left side of the works. The former railway workshops to the left of this line have all been put to other uses, but their frontage in London Street is a preserved architectural feature. The farthest structure in the block, adjacent to the car park is the main works entrance, whose subway can be seen emerging adjacent to the fine drawing office block outside which is stabled the derelict 'Warship' diesel-hydraulic No D818 *Glory*. This locomotive was subsequently repainted and placed on display alongside the turntable only to be unceremoniously cut up in 1985. Built at Swindon, it could have formed an exhibit for the museum which is now to be established on part of the works site.

At bottom left can be seen the cottages of the original railway town, designed by Brunel and Matthew Digby-Wyatt, with the former Mechanics' Institute in the centre. The cottages were, at this time, being restored by Swindon Corporation and finished and unstarted examples can be seen. The work has since been completed and a seedy, run-down area made most attractive.

At the far end of the works the newer red brick structure includes the well known 'A' shop and beyond it is the small yard known as 'the dump'. Here, withdrawn locomotives were stored prior to breaking up. The former Midland and South Western Junction Railway line from Cheltenham to Andover ran across the meadows beyond the works. It closed in the 1960s and by the time of this view its route is impossible to trace. **AC300296**

Waterloo

Here is a grandstand view of the great 21-platform terminus, but it must have been a Sunday for there is little evidence of the intensive 'rush-hour' electric train service into the Southern Region's major station. A solitary Class 50 diesel, waiting with an Exeter train, provides a splash of yellow amid the otherwise deserted platforms, although one or two shorter trains are doubtless hidden under the vast roof. In the foreground, standing on two white arches, is the station's signalbox, displaced by resignalling in the early 1980s, while to the left of the station can be seen the short sidings and lift giving access for rolling stock to and from the Waterloo and City underground line. The 'drain' as it is popularly known, is the only underground operation owned by Network SouthEast, the south east suburban section of BR.

Beyond the terminus, in the shadow of the brown tower block, is Waterloo Eastern, its through platforms serving trains between Charing Cross and the Kent coast. In the background, with red painted piers, is Blackfriars bridge with yellow-fronted electric trains visible in Blackfriars station, immediately on the far bank of the river. The lines from Blackfriars split, the straighter route heading for Herne Hill, while the other line curves round towards London Bridge, where the triangular junction outside Cannon Street (see page 19) can be seen at the very top right.

Returning to Waterloo itself, the area to the left of the station is the proposed site for the terminus of through trains from France via the Channel Tunnel. The choice of site is controversial and this view shows just how small it is.   **AC512015**

Leamington, 1937

A panorama of Royal Leamington Spa in 1937, showing both
stations, with the line towards Banbury heading away to the
top right. The small station to the left is Leamington Spa
Avenue (ex-LNWR), which closed to passengers in 1959. In
this view the GWR station, Leamington Spa General, has
been demolished on the down side and new canopy steelwork
is being erected. The station originally had a Brunelian
timber trainshed which spanned 60ft, and the severed
remains of this are visible on the up platform. The illustration
shows the extent of excavation which was necessary in order
that the entrance to the new steel-framed, limestone-faced
station could be at street level. The signal has dropped and a
down express is departing, as a down local headed by a
Prairie 2-6-2T waits at the far platform. **53218**

Bridgnorth

Once the epitome of a modest Great Western station serving a country town, Bridgnorth nowadays sees more rail passengers in a day than it would have seen in a month when owned by BR. It was an intermediate station on the Shrewsbury-Hartlebury 'Severn Valley' line, a single track cross-country route which closed in 1962. Between Bridgnorth and Shrewsbury the track was lifted and the route abandoned, but preservationists acquired Bridgnorth station and progressively re-opened the line from there to Kidderminster, where a splendid new GWR-style station has been built. Now, as the Severn Valley Railway, it proudly boasts itself 'Britain's premier preserved line', a title with which it is hard to disagree.

This view shows Bridgnorth station fairly early in the preservation period, before the platforms had been lengthened and other modifications made to cope with the large numbers of visitors now received.

The yard is well filled with steam locomotives, some of them rescued from scrapyards and awaiting restoration. Although much restoration work is still being done by the SVR, most of the heavy restoration is now carried out at Bewdley, while Bridgnorth provides maintenance for operational locomotives and the former goods shed is now used for final painting of restored stock. In this view, from the bottom, the locomotives include LMS '8F' 2-8-0 No 8233, the blue-liveried Longmoor Military Railway 2-10-0 No 600 *Gordon*, GWR 0-6-0 No 3205 (now on the West Somerset Railway) BR 'Britannia' 4-6-2 No 70000 *Britannia* (now being restored at Carnforth) and two more GWR tank locomotives.

The footbridge from the station to the main road has since been removed, a most regrettable loss.

AC229387

Stranraer

A brisk sea breeze drives the whitecaps past Stranraer Harbour station as a Sealink ferry disgorges a load of cars. Stranraer Harbour is the Scottish link in the ferry service to Larne in Northern Ireland. Railway promoters were lured to this south west corner of Scotland by the prospect of the short sea crossing to Ireland, Donaghadee being a mere 21 miles across the Irish Sea from the small Scottish harbour at Portpatrick, and distance being particularly important in the days of sail.

The railway reached Portpatrick in 1862, but a branch to serve Stranraer Harbour had been completed a year earlier. Access to Portpatrick by rail and sea was difficult and with the decline of sail its proximity to Ireland became of less importance. By 1874 regular sailings from Portpatrick had ceased and been transferred to Stranraer, where the harbour was in a sheltered location at the foot of Loch Ryan. On the Irish side, Larne then superseded Donaghadee.

In this view of the harbour station, the compact nature of the terminus is readily apparent, the six-car formation of Swindon-built Class 126 diesel units filling the platform.

The Sealink ferry MV *Antrim Princess* was built in 1967 and was one of three ships employed on the route. She carries 1,200 passengers and 155 cars and has a top speed of 19.5 knots. **AC367645**

Docks

Beside the Sea

At the beginning of the 19th century much of 'fashionable' Europe was closed by wars and the wealthy were obliged to look elsewhere for their rest and relaxation. Thus developed the popularity of the spa towns where one could take the waters amid the very best of fashionable, wealthy Britain. From this there followed the development of the coastal resorts with broad promenades and tree-lined avenues designed to bring something of the Mediterranean Riviera to English shores.

Inevitably, these burgeoning resorts quickly sought connection to the developing rail system and as the Victorian era wore on, the development or stagnation of many coastal resorts became closely linked with rail access or the lack of it. The ease of rail access also opened up many of these fashionable resorts to access by the workers of Britain's industrial heartland, such that by the 20th century the annual holiday by the seaside was becoming a regular event for more and more people. The advent of compulsory annual factory shut-downs — in the North the so-called 'wakes weeks' opened the possibility of a seaside holiday to almost all.

The bulk of the transport was provided by rail and those resorts within easy striking distance of major industrial conurbations found themselves changing to cater for a whole spectrum of humanity. The seaside holiday by train lasted into the 1950s and beyond, until widespread car ownership spelt the end. By then, most of the resorts had built a reputation which was unlikely to be affected by a mere change in the mode of travel of their visitors. Perhaps more than any other chapter in this book, 'Beside the Sea' will bring back poignant childhood memories of a very special kind of vacation — without airport lounges, travel sickness or the smell of petrol, but with scents of steam and sea spray and grand vistas of countryside and coastline.

Margate, 1949

Photographed on 12 July 1949, this view of Margate shows a large section of the sea-front, together with the dominant position of the railway station. In this pre-electrification view, ex-SECR coaches predominate and an unidentified 4-4-0 is coupled to one rake in the yard. The station, with its imposing frontage and central tower remains much the same in the 1980s. In this high summer scene the beach is crowded, yet it is little more than three years after the removal of coastal defences. There are at least 28 motor coaches and six double-deck buses in view too, the former doubtless creaming off valuable rail traffic. Like all good Victorian resorts, Margate has a pier and a sea-front entertainment pavilion. **A24854**

Harwich, Parkeston Quay

A fine view of the rail-connected maritime activities at Harwich, Parkeston Quay, established by the Great Eastern Railway and providing North Sea crossings to Belgium, Holland and Denmark. At the bottom of this view is the railway container yard with four overhead gantries to remove the 'boxes' from the flat railway wagons. A large double gantry transfers them to the ship and a freighter in Sealink colours is moored beneath the gantry to await loading. Container traffic has since been transferred to Felixstowe. Parkeston Quay station can be seen with a rake of coaches in one of its two curving platforms. Behind it are immigration offices and customs sheds.

Three ferries are at their berths, the nearest one a Sealink vessel, probably the MV *St George* built in 1968 with a capacity for 1,200 passengers and 220 cars. She was withdrawn in the mid 1970s and sold to Greek owners. Beyond her, with the grey hull and black/red funnel is a ship of the Danish Prinz Line (Harwich-Hamburg/Bremerhaven). The farthest vessel appears to be one of the small, older, Dutch ferries.

The rail freight yards are situated farthest from the camera and a Class 37 diesel is present along with numerous European railway vehicles. The Harwich train ferry slip is illustrated elsewhere in this book.   **AC239263**

Mallaig

The picturesque fishing harbour at Mallaig is situated on the west coast of Scotland. For the first half of the 20th century the railway's had established themselves as the principal transporters of fish. Fast services, often comprising complete trains of special vans, operated from the major fishing ports to move the catches quickly to market. The railway wagons were initially provided with insulation to keep the contents, packed in ice, cool and later versions were refrigerated.

Mallaig was established as a rail-served fishing harbour by the North British Railway, anxious to tap the valuable Scottish herring trade. The 41-mile branch line from Fort William was opened on 1 April 1901, having been engineered by Robert McAlpine & Sons. It included 11 short tunnels and the spectacular Glenfinnan Viaduct, notable as an early use of concrete for such structures.

In this mid-1970s view, rail connection to the quay has gone, as has connection into the stone-built locomotive shed visible to the left of the station. The glass umbrella roof on the station platform is clearly seen, with the small, sturdy granite station building beyond it. Radio signalling has since replaced the semaphores visible in this view, but steam has returned to the line during the summer months with regular workings, usually headed by a preserved LMS 'Black Five' 4-6-0 over the route from Fort William.

The herring shoals, and with them the regular fish trains, have now gone and the small boats in the harbour catch mainly shellfish. The orange vessel moored in the centre of the harbour is Mallaig's 52ft 'Barnett' class lifeboat, since replaced with one of the latest 'Arun' fast afloat lifeboats.   AC324117

Ramsgate, 1920

Kent coastal towns, easily reached from London, were developed initially as fashionable resorts before that same ease of access brought the working masses from London and the home counties. Ramsgate boasted a good fishing harbour and offered sandy beaches, making it a popular choice. The harbour station, seen here in 1920, was a stone's throw from the harbour and immediately adjacent to the promenade and beach. Note the fascinating track layout, with a turntable at the end of the line and a central engine release road. In 1926 the Southern Railway built a 1-mile 48-chain section of line to link Broadstairs and Minster via new stations at Dumpton Park and Ramsgate Town. Ramsgate Harbour station was closed and an amusement arcade now occupies the site, while the promenade seen in this view is now a car park.   **93**

Whitley Bay, 1927

Back-to-back terraces crowd the sea-front at Whitley Bay in this 1927 view. This modest Northeast coast resort is close to the industrial centres on the River Tyne. The North Eastern Railway station has a very neat glazed ridge and furrow train shed. A station roof of this size could be an untidy affair, full of additions and modifications, but Whitley Bay looks smart and well kept. Note the way in which the footbridge is incorporated under the roof, and is provided with matching towers for its goods lift. An imposing clock tower forms part of the station frontage. Whitley Bay is served by trains to Blyth.   **19767**

St Ives, 1937

Each photograph in this chapter is bound to bring back special memories for someone and this view of St Ives is the author's particular favourite. The picturesque fishing village, favoured by artists, was a frequent venue for family holidays some 20 years after this 1937 view was taken. The 4¼-mile branch from St Erth, opened in June 1877, was the last new broad gauge line to be built. The Great Western Railway owned the Tregenna Castle Hotel, and through trains operated to St Ives from Paddington, indeed on summer Saturdays it boasted its own complete 'Cornish Riviera Express' which required three locomotives to take it up the steep bank from the station. Such services ceased by the 1960s, and from 1966 onwards the site of the station was progressively cleared to provide car parking. The fine Cornish granite buildings have given way to a cluster of prefabricated huts some distance up the line, but at least it is still possible to reach St Ives by train, its branch line offering some of the grandest Atlantic vistas to be seen in the UK. A few months after this placid summer scene the village was to be plunged into grief by two lifeboat tragedies in rapid succession, with the loss of both lifeboats and a dozen lives. **PR3644**

Merehead, 1987

In recent years the long-established system of 'wagon-load' traffic serving hundreds of
different customers has largely disappeared and the mixed freight train is almost a thing of the
past. In its place, Railfreight has concentrated on certain selected traffics which lend
themselves to bulk movement by rail. Apart from coal and oil a major source of such traffic is
stone, used mainly in the construction industry and as aggregate for the production of road
coatings. Somerset-based quarrymasters Foster Yeoman are the largest users of rail for stone
shipment and the Company's rail-served quarry is at Merehead, between Frome and Shepton
Mallet in Somerset.

This view, specially taken for this book, shows virtually the entire operation at Merehead
with the 500 acre quarry at the top left. The railway tracks are arranged as a triangle, its apex
in the photograph passing under the Frome-Shepton road and into the quarry loading area.
Here the wagons are loaded by an overhead conveyor system which moves along the length of
the train, filling each wagon in a matter of seconds. Loaded trains, ready for departure, are
then stabled on the lefthand leg of the triangle. The sharply curved righthand side is used for
incoming empties, and on the extreme right can be seen the locomotive shed and workshops.
Here, the wagons are maintained together with the quarry's American-built shunting
locomotive and Yeoman's four Class 59 diesel locomotives (also American-built) which work
the trains to various points in south east England. One of these locomotives can be seen
outside the shed. The BR system is reached by way of the remains of the former Cheddar
Valley line to Witham, seen bottom right, which also connects with the preserved East
Somerset Railway at nearby Cranmore. **CT16813**

Industries

Walton-on-the-Naze, 1920

The Essex resorts of Clacton, Frinton and Walton were as accessible from Northeast London suburbs as the Kent coast was from the Southeast of the city. This slightly damaged view of Walton-on-the-Naze is interesting for being one of the earliest, taken in 1920, and also for including a glimpse of the wing-tip of the biplane from which it was taken. The curved station platform contains a long train of four- and six-wheel coaches headed by a diminutive GER 0-6-0T, while another train of similar vehicles is departing under a column of white steam and smoke. Part of the pier can be seen, together with the groynes constructed across the beach to reduce the scouring effect of the tide, but there are few people on the sand. Walton is today a terminus of 25kV electrified services from Liverpool Street.   **1843**

Morecambe, 1933

The English at play, 1933-style! A beach scene at Morecambe, complete with stalls and sideshows, and most of those on the beach clad in hats and coats, or the men with suits and ties on. On the promenade a mixture of horse-drawn traffic and motor vehicles passes the LMS Promenade station. Morecambe was entirely developed by the railways and had two ex-Midland Railway stations, and a third inherited from the London & North Western Railway. Both MR stations are visible in this view, the original Morecambe station, just below the smoke of a departing train, top centre. Promenade station opened in 1907. The route to the right, towards Heysham is electrified as part of the Lancaster, Morecambe, Heysham electrification at 6,600V dc, dating from 1908. Note the carriage sidings and rather basic locomotive facilities at the Promenade station, also the 'Jinty' 0-6-0T shunting in the goods yard.

42134

Colwyn Bay, 1962

With its North Wales coast line from Chester to Holyhead, the London & North Western Railway served several important resorts, including Rhyl and Llandudno. Between these two lies Colwyn Bay, seen here in 1962, with its station fronting the promenade and close to the pier. The two island platforms are linked by a pedestrian footbridge and a separate goods bridge provided with lifts. The goods yard is reached by a short tunnel under the station forecourt and is deserted in this view, save for a couple of wagons and a lone BR 20-ton brake van. A miniature railway and fairground are squeezed on the narrow strip of ground between the station and goods yard. The predominance of cars and dearth of trains are indicative of the comparatively recent date of this view. **107171**

Blackpool, 1952

The ultimate holiday town and Britain's No 1 seaside resort, totally geared to the working man's annual family break by the sea. As the Aerofilms photographer wings his way over the Blackpool Tower, the 1952 holiday season is in full swing. Crowds throng the Promenade, motor coaches pick their way through the traffic and the crowds, and one of the Corporation's Marton Vambac single-deck trams pauses for custom. In the shadow of the Tower lies Blackpool Central, terminus of the LNWR and Lancashire & Yorkshire Railway joint line from Preston. There are no goods facilities here, just a station dedicated to passenger services and excursion traffic. An LMS 2-6-4T has shut-off steam and drifts towards the station with nine coaches in tow, as a 'Black Five' running tender-first prepares to take out a rake of 10 in BR 'blood and custard' livery. More than 100 motor coaches cram the side streets and yards (top) like some avid collector's Matchbox toys, while the endless rows of back-to-back holiday accommodation are doubtless stretched to the limit to cope with the influx of visitors.   **A47419**

Above:
A bleak scene at Blackpool Central on 24 June 1965 with the tracks filled in and the area used for car parking. The station buildings were being converted into a bingo hall! *R. Fisher*

Minehead, 1930

Minehead is the terminus of a 25-mile long, and very rural, branch line from Taunton. The station was typical of many such GWR branches, except for its very long platform, which was necessary to accommodate the through main line trains which operated to and from Minehead during the summer. This is the view from the sea-front in August 1930 — not a good day as few people have ventured on to the beach. A two-coach 'B' set forming a local service to Taunton stands in the platform while its 2-6-2T locomotive collects a third vehicle from the yard. One of the Great Western's big 70ft corridor coaches with its destination boards on the roof can also be seen. The area to the left of the Strand Hotel was developed as a Butlin's Holiday Camp in the 1950s, and after BR withdrew passenger services to Minehead in 1971 the line was acquired by the West Somerset Railway, which now operates between Minehead and Bishops Lydeard.

Oban, 1949

Our tour of the British coastline brings us to Oban, terminus of the long, tortuous, and breath-takingly beautiful, Caledonian Railway route from Glasgow. This fishing harbour on the Firth of Lorn is the departure point for ferry services to the Isle of Mull and neighbouring islands. In this 1949 view, two long trains stand in the station, and there are plenty of spare vehicles in the yard. Fish vans await loading on the quayside and two lovely fishing boats ride at their moorings. In the background, left, are the pens of the cattle market, and to their right is the locomotive depot. Several locomotives are in steam, including at least one 'Black Five', the mainstay of front rank motive power in the Scottish Highlands. **22629**

Llandudno, 1961

Llandudno is reached by way of a branch from Llandudno Junction. This grand view on
13 June 1961 shows the town centre with the station on its outskirts. The carriage sidings are
well-filled and there is generous covered accommodation over the platforms. The camera is
looking west, with the town dominated by the Great Orme, below which is the pier, with a
steamer departing for the Isle of Man. The summit of the Great Orme is best reached by a
ride on the cable-worked 'tramway' whose Edwardian cars in their dark blue colour scheme
are in perfect accord with the charm of this resort. The large square building (centre left) is
the town's variety theatre. Llandudno is also unusual in that its lifeboat station is situated
some 400yd from the sea. The vessel, *RNLB Lilly Wainwright*, is hauled through the streets
with a special tractor and trailer, and spends much of its time as a prominent feature of the
sea-front, parked at the top of its slipway.   **A90984**

Padstow, 1932

The Southern Railway's lines in Devon and Cornwall were somewhat uncharitably christened the 'Withered Arm'. The westernmost terminus of these SR lines was at Padstow, reached by the North Cornwall Railway in 1899 after painfully slow construction of its route from Halwill Junction had taken some 13 years. Here, in 1932, we see the Padstow terminus on the estuary of the river Camel. The modest passenger station and house combined are dwarfed by the massive fish loading shed built by the Southern Railway in the 1920s. Sidings extend out along the quay, and at least six grounded coach bodies are to be seen. The station handled large amounts of ice and empty boxes in connection with the fish trade, and during the season, up to 1,000 wagons of fish would leave here. After World War 2 the traffic declined sharply, and the goods service was withdrawn earlier than the passenger service which ended in January 1967. Little more than the station house now survives at Padstow. **C18141**

Hayle Wharves, 1938

Little has appeared in print about the short stretch of freight-only branch line from Hayle to Hayle Wharves, and photographs of it are even more rare. That in itself must be good enough reason to include this view of part of that railway leading down beside the Hayle estuary. There seems to be little activity amid the stockpiles and small waterside industries. However, the centrepiece is the distinctive road and rail swingbridge with its standard GWR brick-built signalbox presumably to control not just the bridge, but the complex level crossing over the main A30 road which sits right in the middle of a road junction and two diverging sidings. **59865**

Right:
The crossing at Hayle wharves seen from ground level in April 1950 as '45xx' 2-6-2T No 4504 rushes the steep bank up to the main line with a short freight train. The signalbox seen in the main illustration is visible behind the steam from the locomotive. *B. A. Butt*

Docks

From the very dawn of Britain's railway system, the fortunes of major ports were linked with railway development. The first major railway development, the Liverpool & Manchester, served the city which was then Britain's premier international port, while the later development of the Ship Canal enabled Manchester also to develop as a port. Railways developed to provide vital lifelines to and from the ports at the very time when Britain's international trade was burgeoning — all of it conveyed by sea.

In recent years maritime trade has diminished and long-distance passenger traffic has all but vanished from the oceans around us. Today's ports have changed their shape and character to accommodate bulk cargoes and intermodal traffic. Although the traffic and the scale of operations has changed, most of those major docks which survive continue to make use of their rail connections.

The accompanying illustrations provide a glimpse of the heyday of some of our major ports, whose names became known across the oceans of the world.

Garston, 1934

Garston Dock, situated on the Mersey Estuary upstream from the main Liverpool Docks, remained independent of the Mersey Docks & Harbours Board, having been owned by the London & North Western Railway. Unlike Southampton, with its mixture of freight and passenger liners, Garston was a freight handling dock and this 5 September 1934 view shows that it was almost exclusively rail-served. The vast majority of open wagons in this view are conveying timber, but Garston was also specially equipped for handling Fyffes banana traffic and in a typical year six million bunches could pass through for distribution in the north of England. In the background is the entrance lock, to maintain constant water level in the dock, while the ocean-going freighters are mostly equipped for sheeting-over of deck cargoes. On the extreme left a saddle-tank locomotive is marshalling a string of wagons, and bottom centre, another dock tank is busy with loaded timber wagons. **R320**

Cardiff, 1947

Cardiff was a Great Western port, and this view of the Roath Dock was taken in 1947. Roath Dock opened in 1887, its 33-acre deep water capacity connected to the ocean by way of the Queen Alexandra Dock, reached through the lock at the top left. The berths on the left were for coal shipment, the No 1 conveyor (bottom left corner) having been constructed in the early 1930s. Coal trains reached the dock by way of the ex-Taff Vale Railway sidings at bottom left. At the right-hand quay, two freighters stand alongside the grain sheds, and the modern complex in the foreground is the Spillers mill and silos. Major imports at Cardiff included grain, timber and pit-props, while coal, iron products and general merchandise were exported.   **A7824**

Newport, 1947

A marvellous view of the Great Western's port complex at Newport, with 20-ton coal hoists standing sentinel along the South Dock (top) and the North Dock (centre). Top right is the lock access to the Bristol Channel and at the extreme left of the picture is the River Usk with the famous transporter bridge in the bottom corner. Coal sidings lead along the right-hand side of the North Dock, and the areas of water to the right of these are the timber floating docks with a few rafts of timber in evidence. The timber yards of Nicholas & Co and Burt, Boulton & Haywood occupy the bottom right-hand area, where the rail sidings converge towards East Mendalgief Junction. Two ships are being dry docked on the left, while the 1933 guide shows the land at the top available for letting — by the time of this 1947 view it had still not been taken up.   **A5379**

Southampton, 1923

Perhaps more than any other port, Southampton owes its meteoric development to the railways. The infant Southampton Dock Co, unable to exploit the port's full potential even with the backing of the London & South Western Railway, eventually sold out to that company in 1892. Rapid development then followed and this view taken on 7 August 1923 shows the very heart of Southampton Docks.

This was the heyday of the great trans-Atlantic passenger liners. Rearmost of the vessels in this view is the Cunard liner *Aquitania*, at rest in the Trafalgar dry dock which had opened in 1905, the centenary of the Battle of Trafalgar, and was the largest of its kind in the world until the opening of the King George V dry dock. In the Ocean Dock (centre) are the White Star liners *Homeric* and *Olympic*, the latter a sister ship to the ill-fated *Titanic*. White Star had moved its trans-Atlantic operations from Liverpool to Southampton in 1911, the new dock originally being known as the White Star Dock in their honour. It was from here that *Titanic* had sailed in 1912 on her tragic maiden voyage, her 20 lifeboats woefully inadequate for the 2,200 souls aboard. The extra boats subsequently fitted to *Olympic* are clearly visible.

In the foreground, on the quay which separates the Ocean and Empress docks, boat train coaches can be seen awaiting duty, one of them with a 'B4' class 0-4-0T, built for dock shunting, at its head. Under Southern Railway ownership, the open water area in the background was to be drained and developed as the huge Western Docks complex; work commencing only four years after this photograph was taken. **9074**

Southampton, 1936

A closer view of Southampton's Ocean Dock with the Cunard White Star liner *Aquitania* at berth No 46 on 4 October 1936. The two great shipping companies had amalgamated in 1934. *Aquitania*, known as 'The Grand Old Lady of the North Atlantic' was completed at John Brown's Clydebank yard in 1914 and served until 1949, crossing the Atlantic 475 times and carrying in excess of one million passengers. The workshops of Harland & Wolfe Ltd, whose Belfast yard had built many of the great liners can be seen beyond the ship. On the quay to the right of the dock are the original 1911 terminal buildings which survived until the Ocean Terminal was constructed in the late 1940s. On the extreme right is part of the rail complex serving the extensive freight sheds around the Empress Dock. **R2473**

Barry, 1947

Another view from the 1947 series of South Wales ports, this is a panorama of Barry, looking westwards with Dock No 2 in the centre. The Barry Island branch line enters the picture at bottom right, just beyond Cadoxton station. It skirts the edge of the yard, with its sidings diverging to No 2 dock coal hoists, then swings sharply right through Barry Docks station. Passing off the edge of the picture, through Barry station, the line swings left to cross the causeway, visible (top right) beyond the tank farm to reach Barry Island. A few years after this picture, the Butlin's Holiday Camp was built at Barry Island. Barry Docks were developed by the Barry Railway, Dock No 1 opening in 1889 and No 2, three years later. It passed into the GWR at the Grouping, but despite promotion as a general merchandise port for steamers of more modest proportions, commercial activity there dwindled in postwar years. In recent years Barry Docks have been best known as the location of Woodhams' store of steam locomotives awaiting scrapping. The locomotives were stored on part of the Docks' 108 miles of sidings, much of which has now been lifted. **A7743**

Avonmouth, 1929

Isambard Kingdom Brunel was one of several engineers whose efforts were at one time
channelled into trying to keep the Port of Bristol from silting up. Despite his efforts and
despite its early rail link, Bristol lost its place in the league of major British ports, largely due
to silting at the mouth of the river Avon. Attention turned to developing Avonmouth, with its
direct access to the Bristol channel. This 1929 view shows Avonmouth Dock (centre) with the
Royal Edward Dock at the top right. Very much a general merchandise port nowadays, its
major cargoes are grain, crude chemicals and oil products. These traffics were evident in 1929
also — a large grain mill is seen alongside the quay (top left) and oil storage tanks are visible
at bottom left. In the 1970s a new West Dock was constructed and specialised industries have
taken up accommodation close to the wharves. Most of the traffic through Avonmouth is now
moved by road. The Avonmouth (Old) Dock seen here is now almost surrounded by mills,
while one arm of the Royal Edward Dock is devoted to oil transhipment into adjacent storage
tanks. Despite close links with the GWR, Avonmouth and all the Bristol docks have always
been owned by the City of Bristol.   **19270**

Falmouth, 1947

The Falmouth Docks & Engineering Co retired its last steam locomotive in 1986 having become one of the last outposts of industrial steam in Britain. Falmouth's primary shipping activity is in the repair and dry docking of tankers and cargo vessels, and so it was on 16 August 1947 when the Aerofilms photographer pictured a general cargo steamer and two tankers dry docked there. The port's railway system was mainly used for movement of materials, but the GWR branch from Truro terminated close to the docks. Originally built to broad gauge, it featured several Brunel timber viaducts and the Brunelian terminus station seen in this view. Note that the station's train shed is able to accommodate three standard gauge tracks. This must have been a Sunday or a holiday, for there is little activity, and only a solitary van and a 'Toad' brake van are present in the yard, plus a couple of wagons outside the timber goods shed.

R9232

Holyhead, 1962

In recent years the decline of ocean-going passenger ship operations has led to a shift in emphasis in the passenger rail services to ports. Ocean-liner expresses are now comparatively rare, but the ports serving the English Channel, North Sea and Irish Sea crossings are generally still well served by passenger trains. This traffic was considerably developed during the 1960s with new ferry operators joining BR and its Sealink sector in competition on many routes. This 1962 view of Holyhead shows three contemporary BR passenger ships on the Irish route berthed in the 'V' formed by the quayside station buildings. This arrangement was typical of the cross-platform train-to-ship transfers arranged at such ports. Of interest in this view is the predominence of short ex-LMS coaches — note the 'Jinty' 0-6-0T (bottom centre) moving one rake — which look surprisingly antiquated. Observe too, the third and fourth vessels at the far quay. Adjacent to the large shed is a cargo vessel with rail containers stacked on her decks and to her rear is an antique steam coaster, regrettably unidentified.   **107155**

Harwich, 1952

Another aspect of the link between railways and docks is the operation of train ferry services on which complete railway wagons are shunted directly on to the ship. In the UK such services have been mainly associated with two ports, Dover for the 'short sea route' crossing to Dunkerque, and Harwich with its regular crossings to Zeebrugge. The latter service was originated by the Great Eastern Railway and developed by the LNER. This 1952 photograph of the ferry slip at Harwich shows BR's successor, the 400ft×59ft *Norfolk Ferry* on the Zeebrugge service. Built by John Brown on Clydebank in 1951, she had four railway tracks capable of accommodating up to 35 wagons. In this view the ferry is connected at her stern to the loading 'bridge' with its gantry for raising the ramp according to the level of the tide. On the quay can be seen tank wagons and vans of continental origin — even today comparatively few British vehicles are built for train ferry service. Also in view are a dredger, tugs, coasters and assorted pleasure boats, but also worthy of note are the yards full of Trinity House buoys, standing like the pieces from some elaborate children's board game. Considerable harbour development has taken place at Harwich in recent years with the development of Parkeston Quay and the increase in passenger, container and freight lorry traffic on the southern North Sea crossings, but train ferry operations from here ceased in 1987.   **A43676**

Above:
The MV *Essex Ferry*, sister ship to *Norfolk Ferry*, seen leaving the dock at Harwich. The ferry has four rail tracks and at the time of these photographs the vast majority of the railway rolling stock was provided by continental operators.
British Railways

Burntisland, 1929

In locations where they were unable to bridge wide estuaries, the early railway companies soon became obliged to offer ferry services to provide faster transit times for passengers who would otherwise be faced with a lengthy and round-about journey. The Firth of Forth presented just such an obstacle and the Edinburgh, Perth & Dundee Railway operated six ferry boats on the five-mile crossing between Burntisland and Granton. Burntisland Docks opened in 1876 and passed into the ownership of the North British Railway 20 years later. They were extensively developed for the shipment of coal, which had risen above two million tons per annum by 1910. The 43-acre dock area had nine miles of sidings. This 1929 view shows the main dock area with its breakwaters and entrance locks. The coal hoists are seen in rather more detail than in the 1947 GWR views, and here we can clearly see that the rail yards contain virtually nothing but coal wagons, both loaded and empty. The railway station is visible (centre right) with a saddle tank locomotive running past the signalbox and a 0-6-0 shunting the yard. In the background (top right) we see another port activity not illustrated in earlier views in this chapter, a small shipyard with three vessels under simultaneous construction. Note the sailing coasters and the steamer with the very tall funnel in the dock immediately below the shipyard.

27189

Country Stations

Postwar modernisation, the end of steam, electrification, colour light signalling and a host of other developments have served to change the character of Britain's railways. There are doubtless few scenes in this book which have not changed substantially in the last 30 years. Few of those changes will have been more drastic than those which affected the country railway station.

Once the hub of town or village life, the rural station provided the vital link which connected rural districts together and to the rest of the nation. The country station provided freedom of travel for everyone, regardless of his or her place in the community, and it provided freight transport for goods both into and out of the town.

Increasing rural wealth, car ownership, road improvements and the convenience of lorry transport spelt the end of the country station's prosperity. A single figure, one Dr Richard Beeching dealt the death blow to hundreds of rural stations in his report of 1963 *The Reshaping of British Railways*. Its implementation swept away the country station as it is depicted in the accompanying photographs.

Gobowen, 1956

A grand panorama of a large location, Gobowen, Shropshire in 1956. Here we see almost the complete station layout, controlled by the substantial signalbox at the bottom right. A smaller box controls the level crossing, close to the station. In typical Great Western fashion there are substantial platform canopies and a covered footbridge, while the Italianate station building with white stucco walls is a grand affair. The branch train from Oswestry, a '14xx' class 0-4-2T heading two auto-trailers, is entering the bay platform. Opposite the station is a large farm depot and on the siding are several open wagons probably containing bonemeal fertilizer. This material, from meat processors and slaughterhouses was shipped back to the farms as an inexpensive fertilizer. A lady goods clerk who was responsible for seeing such vehicles loaded, once told me that they frequently contained more maggots than bonemeal! Away from the railway, note the fine old-style petrol filling station near the crossroads, and the new housing estate under construction, top right. **R27217**

Mortimer, 1929

Some of the early railways strove to provide facilities even where there must have been doubt as to whether the traffic would justify them. On the GWR, Brunel adopted a fairly methodical placing of stations at regular intervals, which sometimes necessitated the use of the word 'Road' in the title, as there was no nearby village to provide a name. These 'roadside' stations were built in distinctive styles and because many failed ever to generate viable traffic, few now survive. One which does is Mortimer, on the Reading-Basingstoke line, seen here in 1929. It serves the village of Stratfield Mortimer, part of which is seen in the photograph, together with the Duke of Wellington's stately home at Stratfield Saye. The fine Brunel chalet buildings have been restored to near-original condition, but the goods shed, signalbox and footbridge roof have gone. The station's relative seclusion renders it easy prey for mindless vandalism.   **C18737**

Yatton, 1954

Yatton station, Somerset, in the 1950s. The Bristol & Exeter Railway station buildings here are still in use, but otherwise every vestige of the complex junctions has gone, along with the yard and the huge B&E signalbox. The branch sweeping away to the right was but 2½ miles to Clevedon and closed in 1966. The branch auto-train, formed of two 1950s-built Hawksworth trailers with an 0-6-0PT, is on shed at the right. The Cheddar Valley line diverges to the left, its services usually the preserve of a 2-6-2T and a couple of coaches. Passenger services on this route ceased in 1963 but freight traffic survived a while longer. Beyond the signalbox, an up freight has been 'looped' and its locomotive lets off steam as it waits for the road to Bristol.   **R22264**

Left:
Seen from the down platform at Yatton, a Cheddar
Valley-Bristol train joins the main line on 30 August 1958,
with the former Bristol & Exeter Railway signalbox in the
background. The locomotive is an ex-GWR '4575' class
2-6-2T No 5547 and another of its kind waits behind the
signalbox. *M. B. Warburton*

Moreton-in-Marsh, 1929

A classic country station, and one where the author spent many happy hours in the 1960s, shortly before it was rationalised to leave only the platforms and the much modified remains of its station building. Moreton-in-Marsh is now a crossing place on the long single-track section of the Oxford-Worcester line, between Ascott-under-Wychwood and Evesham. Here, in 1929 we see the station in its full glory. A train of empty wagons bound for Worcester has stopped at the down platform for its ROD 2-8-0 to take water. The sidings in the foreground contain wagons with a variety of loads, and the area in front of them was once the terminus of a horse-drawn tramway.

To the left, the single track branch to Shipston-on-Stour curves away from the station. Motive power was severely restricted on this very lightly engineered branch and was usually a 'Dean Goods' 0-6-0. The locomotive can be seen (top right) beyond the signalbox, having just shunted a string of empty wagons and 'Mex' cattle vans into the siding. The branch mixed train formed of a single coach, a van and a 'Toad' brake van, stands at the platform. Passenger services to Shipston survived only a short while after this view was taken. Note the water tank by the footbridge — it is not often that one sees into the top of such a structure. The timber, Brunel-design goods shed had gone by the 1960s, and the depot building with the tall chimney had been redeveloped as a more modern milk depot. **26880**

Theale, 1947

An interesting view of Theale station, just west of Reading on the West of England main line, in 1947. The large Prestcold building, apparently under construction at this time, is still today a major landmark at this site. It is seen surrounded by derelict single storey structures, probably the remains of some wartime establishment. The fine Brunel chalet station building, demolished in the mid-1960s, is at the bottom left. Adjacent to the timber goods shed is the grounded body of a six-wheel clerestory coach. Open wagons in the goods yard are loaded with both logs and sawn timber, going either to or from the sawmill at bottom left. Only the platforms at Theale now remain, the station having been reduced to unstaffed halt status, and the track layout re-arranged to serve new industrial development. The village has spread across much of the open land in the background, and the main A4 road in the middle distance is now a dual carriageway, paralleled by the M4 motorway, with a complex junction here.   **R9357**

Bembridge, 1938

Probably the ultimate in rural stations was the country branch terminus. This particularly compact example, looking like a minimum space model railway layout, is Bembridge (incorrectly captioned on the original print as Brading) on the Isle of Wight, photographed in 1938. The solitary goods siding contains a brake van, an open wagon, and four vans — note their immaculate white roofs. To save space at the end of the platform a small turntable serves instead of points to allow the locomotive to run round its train. Outside the station, the simple, clean roofs of the buildings at bottom left add to the 'toy town' effect. There is an elaborate horse trough and a scattering of period-piece cars. The beach, visible top left, is deserted. The branch from Brading to Bembridge was closed in September 1953.   **R4644**

Nancegollan, 1963

Rural Cornwall provides the next location, and despite appearances this is a comparatively recent view, dating from 8 July 1963. The station is Nancegollan on the GWR branch from Gwinear Road to Helston. The branch passenger service had been withdrawn in the previous year, but freight — mainly coal and agricultural supplies — was still being moved. Note the immaculate platforms with the standard GWR arrangement of paving round the buildings and cinder or gravel surfacing for the extremities of the platforms. The lack of station nameboards is about the only indication that the station is closed. Beside the coal staithes is a grounded clerestory coach body, a common feature of Cornish stations. The main feature of the goods yard is a large prefabricated provender store. The farm feedstuffs manufacturers were among the few firms who labelled their wagons, and paper stickers can be seen on the sides of several of these vans. The resurfaced road without its white lines is a noticeable feature, as is the culvert giving access to the farm at bottom right.   **A116724**

Above:
On 14 April 1960, ex-GWR '45xx' 2-6-2T No 4552 shunts wagons for brocolli traffic in Nancegollan goods yard.
P. Q. Treloar

Princetown, 1952

Still in the West Country, here we have a complete branch terminus, at Princetown, Devon. The remote terminus of the branch which twisted its way up over the moors is best known for its connections with that most forbidding of high security prisons, Dartmoor. The stone-built station structures provide a compact terminus with goods yard facilities, cattle dock, engine shed, coaling and watering, and permanent way stores. With just three open wagons in evidence, clearly the facilities were more than adequate for the traffic on offer. The steep, sharply curved branch was worked by small-wheeled Prairie tanks of the '44xx' class, and its passenger service was withdrawn in March 1956.   **R16164**

Church Fenton, 1953

South west of York, on the line to Leeds and Doncaster, lies the village of Church Fenton. Here we have an instance of a country station which became important because of its strategic location at a divergence of routes. Quite possibly at such locations there might have been insufficient local traffic or population to warrant a station at all, but the gradual development of rail routes converging on one point produced their own reason for the development of a station. The main line to York runs straight, from bottom to top of the photograph. The double track from Leeds emerges from the lower left, and the route to Harrogate sweeps away to the left at the top. Work is in progress on the platform canopies which have part of their covering missing, while the ramps from the footbridge appear to have been reconstructed. Note the separate signalboxes controlling the junctions at either end of the station, and the interesting arrangement of the booking office, close to but not actually on the over-line road bridge. The station remains in use but much of the complex trackwork has gone, together with the manual semaphore signalling and the modest goods yard.   **R18284**

Morpeth, 1927

'Railway station, country town, Morpeth' reads the caption to this fine view of the splendid station provided in this Northumberland town. Situated on the East Coast main line, Morpeth was the junction for lines diverging towards Blyth on the coast, and inland to Reedsmouth (closed in 1952 to passenger traffic). The fine station building has extensive platform canopies. This view shows some splendid lorries delivering to and from the large goods shed on the right. At the top an 0-6-0 is backing on to the small turntable to be turned before taking out the 12 wagons which it has just marshalled. Vehicles lettered 'LMS' and 'NE' are clearly visible. There are five cattle wagons standing at the loading dock, and further along the same platform an open wagon is being unloaded with the aid of an improvised ramp. The cattle market is close by, on the extreme right of the picture. **19776**

Warminster, 1937

All the vital ingredients of a country town station are seen again in this view of Warminster, Wiltshire, in August 1937. This Great Western station is nowadays part of the Southern Region, but the station building and shelter remain much as they are seen here. Sadly, the covered footbridge, the shed, signalbox and goods yard have all gone. A GWR 2-6-0 heading a short freight to Westbury has paused in the loop behind the footbridge. Private owner wagons, including vehicles owned by Oxcroft and the Co-operative Wholesale Society (CWS), and LMS open wagons fill the yard. Beside the Brunelian 'broad gauge' timber goods shed stand two GWR delivery lorries and another is parked by the station entrance. The agricultural facilities in the foreground are noteworthy. Chemical drums have been off-loaded into a compound, while the small cattle dock is provided with direct access to the extensive cattle market with its scrupulously clean pens. Dart & Son, Auctioneers and Valuers, have their sign displayed on the roof of the black shed. Note the two bogie well wagons with their strange tunnel-shaped loads.   **54760**

Brent, 1957

Today's IC125s make light work of the South Devon banks, but in steam days they were a formidable obstacle, particularly if the train was required to stop at one of the wayside stations. Brent, nowadays marked only by the remains of its signalbox and goods shed (neither now used for its intended purpose), was once the junction for Kingsbridge, and was a modest country station in its own right. This view is looking south with the Exeter-Plymouth main line passing left to right, and the gradient in the same direction. The station is a post-broad gauge rebuild with two through tracks, and the branch served from the outer face of an island platform. The downgraded corridor coaches forming the Kingsbridge train can be seen in the platform. The buildings are all brick-built in the standard Great Western style for the final years of the 19th century.   **R29314**

Tavistock, 1928

Tavistock, Devon, was one of those towns with the dubious luxury of more than one station. These quirks of Britain's haphazard railway development frequently resulted in rivalry between differing railway companies, or were the result of such rivalry. They frequently left a legacy of difficult interchange (at Tavistock the GWR and SR stations were a mile apart) and in many instances such towns are now without any station. Here, is Tavistock South (the GWR station, despite its name!) in 1928 with its broad gauge era Brunelian structures in all their glory. The distinctive train shed was a replacement for a similar original one, destroyed by fire, and remained in use until the station closed in December 1962. Note how the legacy of broad gauge dimensions allows for three standard gauge tracks through the station and two through the goods shed. I visited the site in the mid-1960s to find it all still intact. One interesting feature visible at the top end of the far platform, is the wagon weighbridge, with its hip-roofed hut. The weighing table can be seen in track behind the platform, and a short piece of interlaced track was provided to enable trains to bypass the weighing machinery when necessary. General merchandise wagons including a milk tank stand in the yard, while two cranes of differing capacities (the larger of the two being a standard GWR 6-ton crane) are provided. Extensive traffic in timber is evident. Nothing now remains at this site.   **23606**

Stone, 1929

The fine North Staffordshire Railway station at Stone was photographed in 1929. The two-storey structure, no doubt with living accommodation upstairs, stands in the fork of the main Colwich-Stoke line with the diverging route to Norton Bridge. A mixed goods train is emerging from the yard and heading for Stoke. On the main line an up goods train has stopped to shunt, leaving the brake van and a dozen wagons in the platform. The rest of the train is setting back to drop off some coal wagons in the yard, but the locomotive is just off the picture. Note the logs awaiting loading with a small crane, and at the extreme left a gated private siding to a kiln, doubtless to allow clay deliveries by rail, pottery manufacture being the county's major industry at this time. **26983**

Silloth, 1929

The station with the pretty glazed timber screen along its platform is Silloth, on the Solway Firth. This small station was terminus of the North British Railway branch from Abbey Holme. A sunny day in 1929 found the village shops with their canvas sunblinds out and a fair amount of activity. The old 0-6-0 is waiting to depart with its three-coach train, there are pedestrians crossing the yard by way of the open, gateless crossing which cuts right through all the loop sidings, and there are figures on the bowling green. Silloth was a modest seaside resort, but also had industrial activity with two docks through which raw materials were supplied to a flour mill and a fertiliser plant. The outer (Marshall) dock opened in 1856, and by the time of this photograph, was silting up, while the inner (New) dock was opened in 1885. Both were rail-served by the sidings which passed beyond the station, the white staining visible on the ground being evidence of the loading of fertilisers. The single-storey station building was original, but the glazed draught screen was a subsequent addition. In the mid-1950s the branch was dieselised as part of the Lake District dieselisation programme, but closed to passengers in September 1964.   **27450**

Trains in the Landscape

Those who love railways would always argue that the presence of a railway actually enhances a scene, whatever its natural attractions. In the rugged beauty of the Aberglaslyn Pass, what railfan has not paused to imagine a Welsh Highland narrow gauge train clinging to its ledge on the mountainside, or dreamt of a Lynton and Barnstaple train wending its way through the tree-covered slopes approaching Lynton? Who can travel through our industrial heartland and not mentally turn the clock back to the days when a steam locomotive lumbered past every few minutes with 50 wagons of coal in tow?

Environmentalists might frown upon the view that the railway is anything but an ugly scar on the landscape, but compared to the broad, white eyesore of main road or motorway, the narrow ribbon of steel on its dark brown ballast could scarcely be any less obtrusive. Seen from the air, the train adds action and movement to the scene which would otherwise be a dull still-life, scarcely worth bothering to photograph.

Lickey Incline, 1946

No selection of photographs of Britain's railways would be complete without a view like this, of the legendary Lickey Incline, between Bromsgrove and Barnt Green on the ex-Midland Railway route from Gloucester to Birmingham. The tranquility of the Worcestershire countryside is rent asunder by the efforts of an LMS 4-6-0, in less than perfect condition, with steam coming from every orifice, to lift its train up the gruelling two miles of 1 in 37 on Britain's steepest main line gradient. At the rear, two '3F' 0-6-0Ts are giving a hearty shove, one of them with steam to spare, but you can bet that speed is down to walking pace. The whole ensemble is in LMS livery in this early postwar view.   **R7593**

Southall, 1931

In the 1930s the Great Western Railway's 'Cheltenham Flyer' held the record as the world's fastest train for a short period. This view of the GWR main line at Southall in that period shows a short express train (not thought to be the 'Flyer') headed at speed by what appears to be one of G. J. Churchward's straight-footplated 'Saint' class 4-6-0s. It is running on the down fast line and has just crossed the skew iron bridge, well known today for its road traffic jams.   **35001**

Oakham, 1954

A classic panorama of a Midland line freight service, featuring the coal workings between Notts/Derby and London. Here, another Beyer-Garratt locomotive heads a train of 66 empty wagons through Oakham, the county town of England's smallest county, Rutland, on 26 August 1954. The locomotive is visible (top right) and its train is formed of both hopper and conventional coal wagons, returning to the Nottingham area from Brent. Oakham's ex-Midland Railway station is seen to good advantage and had coal staithes, cattle pens and a large goods shed. The signalbox (top right, beyond the station) is well-known as the one on which the former Airfix plastic model kit was based.   **R21541**

The 'Devon Belle', 1947

The caption details provided on many of these Aerofilms prints are delightfully vague and this view is simply titled 'Exeter'. It shows the Waterloo-Ilfracombe all-Pullman 'Devon Belle' in the Devonshire countryside. The locomotive is one of Bulleid's streamlined 'West Country' class 4-6-2s wearing the Southern Railway triple-lined livery. The 12-coach train is formed as follows: two parlour cars, kitchen car, two parlour brakes, kitchen car, three parlour cars, kitchen car, parlour car, observation car. Two observation cars were required for the 'Devon Belle' and were turned at the end of each journey. I well remember, during holidays at Ilfracombe, watching the car being turned on the turntable there. The 'Devon Belle' was short-lived; the luxury, meals-at-every-seat, service quickly becoming uneconomic as road transport eroded the railway's business throughout the 1950s. **A7651**

Above:
Wearing early BR livery 'West Country' 4-6-2 No 34017 *Ilfracombe* is the perfect choice of locomotive for the all-Pullman Waterloo-Ilfracombe 'Devon Belle', seen here near South Molton Road station on 2 August 1952.
A. C. Cawston

LMS Beyer-Garratt, 1948

From luxury passenger to heavy freight, and an unusual view of an LMS Beyer-Garratt 2-6-0+0-6-2T passing Kilworth in 1948. The Midland Railway main line from London to Derby was laid out with four tracks to enable express services to avoid hold-ups behind the endless succession of slow coal trains which abounded on this route. Midland locomotive policy had meant that for may years the 0-6-0 wheel arrangement had been standard for goods engines, necessitating double-heading on heavy trains. The Beyer-Garratt design aimed to economise by having, effectively, two locomotive chassis supporting a single boiler and operated by a single crew. In this view the locomotive is operating forwards, with its water tank leading and the steam-operated rotary coal bunker to the rear. The patched-up array of ex-private owner, pooled coal wagons on this train bound for Brent from the Notts/Derby coalfield are worthy of note.   **A14279**

Floods near Olney, 1951

The '4F' 0-6-0 was typical of the legacy of the Midland's small engine policy, and hundreds of such locomotives soldiered on through the BR period, almost to the end of steam traction. Here, in early BR black livery a '4F' heads a freight train across desolate and flooded countryside near Olney, 10 miles west of Bedford on the line to Northampton. This Midland Railway route sported a fine four-arch bridge over the River Ouse, which has burst its banks, leaving the railway embankment as a narrow causeway and a vital lifeline. The photograph was taken in 1951 and passenger services over the Bedford Midland Road-Northampton Bridge Street line were withdrawn in March 1962, shortly before the Beeching Report.

A34573

Kent hop fields, 1936

The hop farms of Kent employed vast numbers of seasonal workers for harvesting and until the early 1960s many of these workers would be brought in by train from the east London suburbs. In this 1936 view at an unrecorded location, four locomotives return light through a landscape of hop vines after heading 'hop picker's specials'. All ex-South Eastern & Chatham Railway types, they are from the left, '01' class 0-6-0 No 1371, 'C' class 0-6-0 No 1037, 'D' class 4-4-0 No 1742 and 'C' class 0-6-0 No 1582. Such locomotives survived to relative antiquity on this type of service, finally bowing out with the spread of electrification in the early 1960s. **R2275**

LMS '2P', 1923

This chapter concludes with four views of trains in motion. There is little to be said about them individually so they have been grouped together. Such shots must have taxed the photographer's skill, particularly when the aircraft was not actually following and 'pacing' the train. In the first view we swoop low over LMS '2P' 4-4-0 No 776 at speed between Burton and Derby. The second vehicle is an ex-Midland 12-wheel dining car.　　　**20859**

Dover Boat Train, 1937

A fine view of an 11-coach Southern Railway express, simply captioned 'Dover boat train' headed by 'Schools' class 4-4-0 No 921 *Shrewsbury*. This shows to advantage a complete train of the Maunsell era with his typical olive green main line corridor coaches headed by one of the very successful 'Schools' locomotives. Catering facilities are provided by the Pullman kitchen car fifth vehicle from the rear of the train.　　　**R3711**

Diesel-electric No 10000, 1949

The Midland's four-track main line was a popular hunting ground for the Aerofilms photographer, perhaps because it was near to the firm's Elstree base. Here, in 1949, he captures the LMS/English Electric main line diesel-electric prototype No 10000 bursting out of the shadows near Radlett with a 10-coach express. This medium-power 1,600hp locomotive (Type 3 in current categories) lasted little more than a dozen years in service but proved its worth, and when worked in multiple with sister locomotive No 10001 was capable of operating heavy expresses over the West Coast route. This section of the Midland main line was electrified with 25kV overhead system in the early 1980s. **R23166/49**

Above:
The pioneer main line diesel-electric locomotive No 10000, built by English Electric for the London Midland & Scottish Railway and delivered shortly before Nationalisation in 1948. *Ian Allan Library*

Railcar, Newbury, 1953

Another early diesel, and another example of an 'economical' recording of the location, for this view is simply captioned 'Rail car, Newbury'. The vehicle is one of the final series of Great Western Railway AEC diesel railcars built in the early 1940s, and appears to be No W21. It wears the BR carmine and cream livery applied during the 1950s. Two single track lines served Newbury, the erstwhile Didcot, Newbury & Southampton Railway and the Lambourn Valley branch. Opened as the Lambourn Valley Tramway between Newbury and Lambourn in 1898, it was taken over by the GWR and became a typical rural branch line. Heavy traffic in racehorses from Lambourn prompted the GWR to develop a diesel car capable of hauling several horseboxes and the experimental car No 18 became known as the Lambourn Valley car. Subsequent cars differed in outline but were also capable of working this traffic when required. The Lambourn branch closed to passengers in 1960 but remained used for military traffic between Newbury and Welford Park until 1973.   **A52879**

Industries

British industrial development and the development of the railways went hand in hand throughout the Victorian era and the early years of the present century. The pick-up freight train and what is nowadays called 'wagon-load traffic' enabled even quite small industries to be successfully served by rail with the occasional incoming wagon of materials or an outgoing wagon of finished products. Heavy and bulky commodities established the best partnership with rail, for until reliable and powerful road lorries came along there was really no other way to move them other than by slow canal and river transport.

Industries such as coal, steel and minerals now provide the major part of BR freight traffic but in the accompanying historic views we see a variety of lineside rail-served industries. The unique aerial viewpoint enables us to have an overall view of some quite large industrial complexes which were once the very heart of local communities.

Staines, 1928

Staines in Middlesex was the birthplace of linoleum floor covering, a material which until the development of vinyl in the 1960s was the universal flooring in homes and businesses throughout the land. This 1928 view shows the Staines Linoleum Manufacturing Co's factory. Running downwards from the top right is the Metropolitan Water Board siding which was closed in the 1930s. Through the centre, horizontally, runs the Staines-Windsor line of the Southern Railway, with Staines Central station off the picture to the right. Staines West (GWR) station is visible on the left with its goods shed and curved siding full of coal wagons. From this yard a single track crosses the dark line of the Wyrardisbury river to enter the lino factory. It passes through buildings and eventually emerges in a yard area, complete with wagon turntables and a connection leading up to the SR line. Once inside the works, wagons were shunted by an industrial tractor. The company had two special GWR wagons which worked between Staines and Smithfield. The factory closed during the 1960s, the area north of the railway now being a housing estate and that to the south being an industrial park with warehouses and factories, none of it rail-served. Staines West station was converted to offices in 1981. **23491**

Buildwas, 1964

Merry-go-round coal traffic to power stations is nowadays synonymous with Railfreight, and this is one of the main bulk commodities which rail transport has dominated for many years. Much of the movement of coal to power stations was until quite recently carried in traditional open wagons of under 20-ton capacity, many of the older ones wooden-bodied. This view shows Buildwas power station on the banks of the River Severn, with Buildwas station just off the lower right-hand side. Loaded wagons can be seen waiting to discharge their loads into the conveyors which feed the station's furnace houses. The power station has its own rail system for the removal of ash, and a very tight radius return loop is to be seen in the foreground. In the mid-1960s following the closure of the adjacent Seven Valley railway line, this power station became known as Ironbridge 'A', and a new 'B' power station served by Merry-go-round coal trains was opened on the site of the former passenger station.   **A134697**

Seaham, 1934

Railways and steam traction were born in the collieries of Northeast England, but in their earliest days the railways were still only used to move coal as far as the nearest navigable waterway. The family of the Marquis of Londonderry owned a number of small coal mines in the Penshaw area, and wagonways carried their coal to the River Wear. Instead of building a railway to the Wear however, it was decided to build a line directly to the nearest point on the coast, at Seaham, and to build a harbour there. Work commenced in November 1828 and the first coal was shipped through the harbour in July 1831. This view shows a colliery on the coast at Seaham in 1934. At least one colliery shunter is seen at work amid the lines of wooden-bodied open coal wagons. Note too, that rail transport is used to convey waste material to the tip — straight over the cliff into the sea — environmentally anti-social even in the 1930s, one would have thought! **P45962**

Ellesmere Port, 1949

A large timber yard at Ellesmere Port, seen in 1949. A small industrial steam crane is moving a twin bolster wagon — two four-wheel wagons, each with its own bolster, semi-permanently coupled — on private sidings between vast stock-piles of imported timber. The cut timber has probably come from Canada, where these large timber sections, 24-30ft long are nicknamed 'British Columbia toothpicks'. The timber lengths would span the bolsters of a pair of wagons for rail movement to a timber mill where they would be sliced up to workable dimensions. Note the variety of shades, the darker timbers being hardwoods and treated timbers.　**27863**

Warrington, 1934

Identification of this view has proved difficult, its caption simply reading 'Warrington, 1934', but it is Padgate on the ex-Cheshire Lines Committee line from Manchester-Liverpool. The area around the station has seen much development since this view, but Monk's store yard for pipe sections is still there. In this photograph the yard itself is not rail-served, though a rail-mounted crane is provided with its own isolated length of track. Materials arrive in open wagons and must have been tripped by lorry from stockpiles in the station yard. The scrapyard in the foreground has a rail connection and sidings leading to the various buildings. Note the rather grand and immaculate passenger station and the rural nature of its surroundings.　**44423**

Miscellany

In this section I have had to group together three unrelated aspects, the first two of which relate to entertainment. We see travelling shows, fairs, placed close to a railway station in the days when the majority of patrons would be travelling by rail. Under 'Minor Railways' we see rail transport used for entertainment primarily, rather than in any serious transport role. Finally, a couple of accidents support the rather cynical viewpoint that some of the population find such things a bizarre form of 'entertainment'.

Durham, 1948

This photograph required more than the usual degree of detective work, for the caption 'Durham — 1948' clearly does not tell the whole story. Certainly this is not the main Durham station, rather it appears to show a small branch station — either Elvet or Sherburn House on the branch from Pittington. The signalbox stands astride the end of the platform, and a small turntable can be seen. In the background flows the River Wear, and the huge public event is most probably the Durham Miners' Gala. The fair boasts some big rides including J. Powell & Sons Supreme Speedway and Alf Harker's Moonrocket. The Elvet branch closed to passengers in 1931.   **A17417**

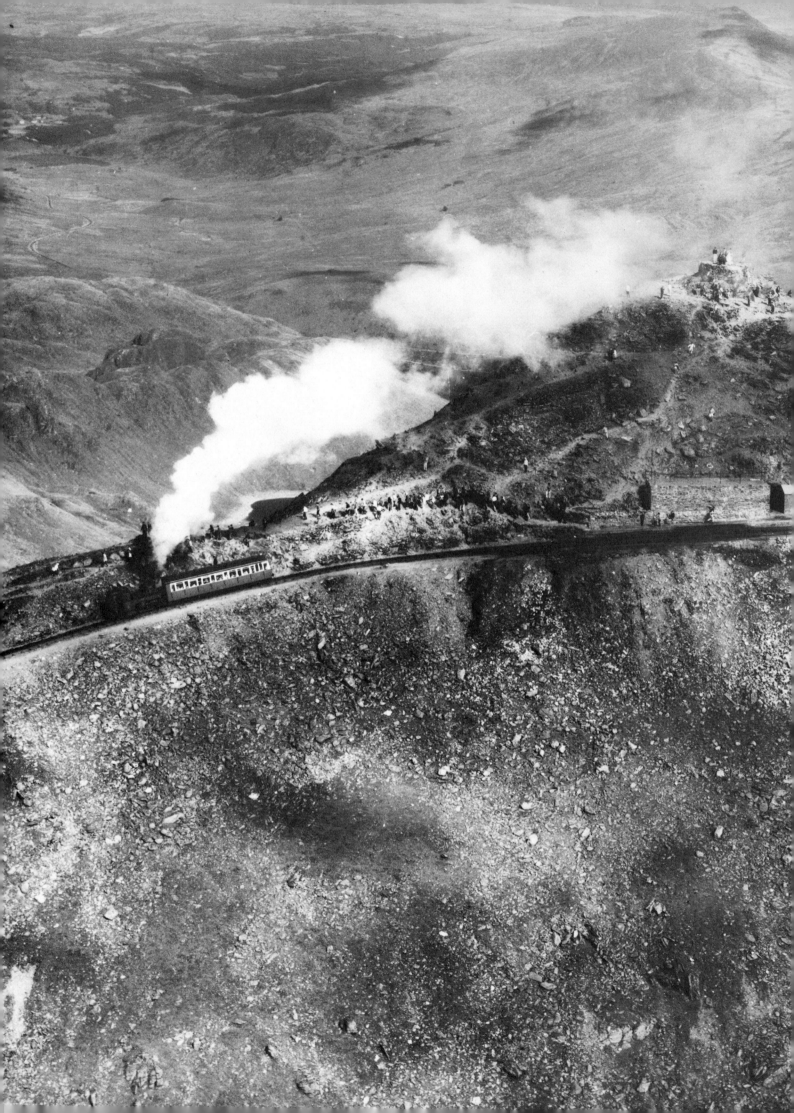

Snowdon, 1965

Built purely for the entertainment of tourists, the Snowdon Mountain Railway, from Llanberis to Snowdon Summit, opened in 1897. It is operated on the Swiss Abt rack system having a toothed centre rail which engages a cog on the underside of the engine, and is of 2ft 7½in gauge. It remains to this day the only rack mountain railway in the British Isles. This view shows the Summit station, with a train just starting the descent. A large crowd is awaiting return trains and some have gathered on the summit itself, 3,561ft above sea level. The weather on this occasion was unusually clear; for much of the time the summit is enveloped in cloud. **153541**

Below:
A prewar view of the Snowdon Mountain Railway, showing the open-sided coaches then in use. Locomotive No 6 *Padarn* waits with an ascending train at Clogwyn, the last station before the summit, to be passed by No 8 *Eryri* which is approaching with a descending train. Nos 6 and 8 belong to the batch of three locomotives delivered in 1922/23, which differ in design from the earlier locomotives.

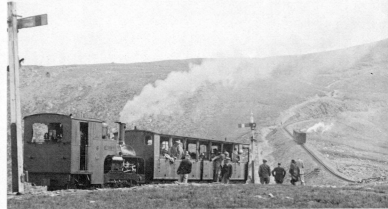

Dymchurch, 1949

Here are two views of the world's smallest public railway, The Romney, Hythe & Dymchurch which runs for 13½ miles across the Romney Marshes to Dungeness, to terminate close by the lighthouse and the nuclear power station. It was conceived as a main line railway in miniature and a run behind one of its Gresley-style 4-6-2 locomotives is an exhilarating experience. The first view shows two trains passing at Dymchurch station. Despite the mere 15in gauge, the scene is complete with covered station, signalbox, water tower and footbridge.   **A22984**

Dymchurch, 1953

The RH&DR was conceived by Capt J. P. Howie and its first locomotives were designed by the legendary model engineer Henry Greenly. It was opened to traffic in 1927 and has served as a local carrier operating school trains, etc. Indeed, during World War 2 its 'front-line' position on the Channel coast led to the operation of a miniature armoured train with anti-aircraft weapons. In this 1953 view a train of four-wheel coaches rattles across the marshes near Dymchurch.   **19051**

'Benny', 1948

Inventors have always been fascinated by the possibility of railways which would be cheaper to build or faster, or would overcome some of the engineering problems of conventional railways, and one such was the monorail. George Bennie's propeller-driven system was set up as a short experimental section above the LNER branch to Milngavie near Glasgow. This 1949 view, captioned with a mispelling, shows the monorail car at its terminus. The railway lasted from 1930 until 1956, but Bennie was unable to attract investment in a system which would have required thousands of tons of structural steelwork in every mile. **19572**

Right:
The Bennie Railplane was heralded as an entirely new form of transport which could be built over existing railway lines to offer a high speed passenger service. The vehicles were driven by airscrews mounted fore and aft, and the experimental installation at Glasgow was the only one ever built. *Topical Press Agency*